9/19/11

To:

You are blessed
and Highly
Favored by God

Is That Man...
Your Husband?

Ms. Michelle

Bloomington, IN Milton Keynes, UK

authorHOUSE™

AuthorHouse™
1663 Liberty Drive, Suite 200
Bloomington, IN 47403
www.authorhouse.com
Phone: 1-800-839-8640

AuthorHouse™ UK Ltd.
500 Avebury Boulevard
Central Milton Keynes, MK9 2BE
www.authorhouse.co.uk
Phone: 08001974150

First published by AuthorHouse 6/20/2006

ISBN: 1-4259-3820-5 (sc)

Unless otherwise noted, Scripture quotations are from The King James Version of the Bible.

Printed in the United States of America
Bloomington, Indiana

This book is printed on acid-free paper.

Dedication

To my Husband TO BE ... Although I have not been made aware of who you are in the natural realm, and I am not certain where you are geographically, I know that God is preparing you to receive me, And under no uncertain terms, when the appointed time is made manifest, you will be perfectly designed to Love, Nurture, Encourage, Protect and Comfort me. You are the only man besides Christ who has the authority to love me without boundaries, yes ... even as Christ hath loved the church and gave his life for it. You will gladly and with ease treat me as wonderful as you treat your own body, seeking the best for me at all times. I will trust safely in your ability to make decisions, because you are prudent in the consideration of our future. You are confident and secure therefore you will celebrate my wisdom, consider my words, and boast of my accomplishments, knowing and understanding that you are joined to a Virtuous Woman. You have excelled in righteousness and you are clothed with Authority, Strength, Faithfulness and Love. You have been crowned with honor by God, and named a Mighty Man of Valor. You possess the Power, Grace and Favor to cover your household, always administering wise counsel to your queen. You are filled with the Word of Life through Jesus Christ and when I drink of the living water that flows from your belly, I will never thirst again. I long for the pleasure of becoming one with YOU, but I will wait patiently for YOU, because YOU, My Brother ... Are worth the wait.

Ms. Michelle

Acknowledgments

I praise God for all of the wonderful people that contributed to my experiences in writing this book. *First to my Lord and Savior Jesus Christ* who pulled me out of bondage and gave me courage coupled with the uncanny ability and talent to write. To my beautiful, talented and intelligent daughter, *Stephanie Raychelle Thompson* who endured my sitting up late hours of the night pecking away on the computer while she was trying to sleep. To *Evangelist Betty Williams,* the humble vessel that God used to call this book out of my spirit and into manifestation during my attendance at the **W**omen **A**nointed **S**anctified and **H**oly (**W.A.S.H.**) Retreat, founded by *Evangelist Doris Turrentine*. To my most creative and witty friend *Gospel Comedian/Pastor,* *Broderick E. Rice* who gave me the inspiration for the book title, your words and insight significantly impacted this book and my life. Very Special thanks to my Mom, *Helen Payne* who graciously allowed me to retreat in her home while writing and gathering the funds to publish this book, thanks for peeping in on me from time to time and for caring enough to prepare breakfast, lunch and dinner for me when I was so involved with writing that I neglected to take a break from writing, to feed myself (smiling). My gratitude is extended to my friend and Brother, *Pastor John A. Edwards*, for praying with and for me to stay focused during my season of becoming an Author. Special thanks to *Brother Ennis Woods* for encouraging me to write from my heart, sharing the real story in raw form. Thank you, *Bishop Clinton House and First Lady Mary House* for sound spiritual leadership, teaching me by example that *"I can do all things through Christ which Strengtheneth me."* To my personal assistant, **Ms. Robbye Wright**, thanks for having my back in good times and in trying times, you are my sister in the Lord and I want to thank you for taking the time to read through my manuscript before it was published, and for speaking encouraging words to me as though it were already named a national best seller. To **Alfred Wooden** for always being there to lend a helping hand with a willing heart. To **Mrs. Carrie Brock-Phillips** who always freely gives unconditional support and encouragement with an uncompromised expectation for God's best.

To **Mr. Jerry A. Watson** for your heart-wrenching role in pushing me to the next level in my ministry and my personal walk with God. Though your heart and your true intent towards me yet remains a mystery, I conclude through the love of Jesus Christ that you are a wonderful, intriguing and exciting man of God. To my niece, **Mrs. Tiffini Birkett** thanks for being my number one fan, and for loving me just for me. Your character exemplifies the epitome of compassion and has inspired me to reach for the very heart of God. To my big brother **Minister Antonious Thigpen** for ministering support and encouragement to me in the final stages of this manuscript and for being so willing to sacrifice your time and energy to help me walk into my destiny as an author. To my best friend **Ms. Sheila Coleman** thanks for putting up with me for well over 30 years as I continued to burn your ears with the vision that God had given. You have always believed in me against all odds, and celebrated with me on each level, I love you for it. Thank you to everyone at **AuthorHouse**, for treating me and my work with respect and dignity. And ... finally *to my husband to be*, whoever you are and where ever you are, when you read this book, you will know where I have been, you will understand who I am and how to love me.

Gods Best To You All
Ms. Michelle

Table of Contents

RECOMMENDED FOR READING

This book is written and recommended for reading:

- To those, who are purpose driven, it will inspire you.

- To my virtuous sisters who possess the natural ability to love, this book will empower you.

- To my Brothers who understand and are willing to embrace the opportunity to love a woman, especially those who are faithful and responsible enough to be a Husband, this book will enlighten you.

- This book is a **"MUST READ"** to Pastors and Leaders, Chapter 2 will bless you. *Please note that if you are a Pastor or leader with ill motives and live according to your own agenda, Chapter 2 will SHINE LIGHT on your behavior because it will EXPOSE YOU.

    ... And finally to the countless thousands of scattered souls who have been hurt in our churches and in relationships this book will encourage and uplift you.

God's best In Your Life
Ms. Michelle

My Dearest Ms. Michelle,

It was at a Greyhound Bus Depot sometime in the late 80's where it all began; a journey of destiny for you and I. I had no idea at the time what would become of us both individually or corporately, but now just look what the Lord had in mind and only you and I know all of what that means. Maybe that will be for a book that we will write together at another time.

Congratulations for making the choice to be a victor and not a victim, to be a winner and not just a wisher, a walker and not just a talker. I am so Godly proud of you and indebted to you for your encouragement, love and support. Continue to pursue your purposed path and soon the world will be all the better because you did. I love you now and I always will.

Eternally enriched,
Broderick E. Rice

www.BroderickRice.org

Forward

*J*s that Man your Husband,

The Book you are about to read, goes to the heart, of
societal misfortune It demonstrates how by standing with
God and ones personal moral convictions God can prove
his righteousness among men. I trust that you will rejoice,
cry and identify with every line as she shares the sometimes
painful, but revealing life surrounding a failed marriage, but
in the end she ultimately proves that if you live right and
triumph over temptation God will use your life to inspire
others.

Emory B. James, Senior Pastor
Ephesians New Testament Church, Fontana, California

Words of Inspiration about the Author

- A friend loveth at all times, and a brother is born for adversity. (Proverbs 17:17).
- Webster defines friend as one attached to another by affection; an intimate associate; a supporter.

Michelle has been that friend to me in every sense of the word. Her life has been one of hopes, dreams, aspirations, faith, drive, encouragement and yes, even some disappointments. Her life and experiences have had a positive influence in my life, and here is just one of the many reasons why. Later in Chapter 5 you will read about Michelle's experience/relationship with her **former** church/pastor. Unknown to either of us at the time, we were experiencing similar storms. You see, Michelle had moved away from Las Vegas to attend college. While she was away, there were times that we spoke only twice a year, once on her birthday and again on my birthday! *(This to me is a sign of true friendship! When you can talk to a person twice a year and pick up like you spoke with one another the day before.)* Michelle was freed from bondage and God released her to come back home. It was at that time that we had the opportunity to share and glean from one another. The covenant friendship that was formed when we were 5 years old was reaching another dimension. It was during that season in my life that Michelle ministered to my soul. She shared with me the storm that God had brought her through, and reminded me that God is not a respecter of persons. I could go on and on about how this woman of God has blessed me personally and all those that are blessed to be around her. Michelle has the "gift of gab!" and lives to uplift and encourage people. She has a knack for reminding people of who God says they are! Michelle has faced many obstacles in her life. However, we could all take a page from her book of faith and perseverance. I know that the readers will be blessed by this book, as I have been time and time again blessed by her friendship.

Sheila Coleman

~~~~~~~~~~~~~~~~~~~~~~~~~~~~~~

Ms. Michelle is a great woman of God, excellent preacher/teacher of the Word and a definite role model for young people. This book is a must read, because today many of us seem to be much more interested in having a church with air condition, but in this manuscript Ms. Michelle profoundly expresses her concern about the churches prayer condition...

John A Edwards Pastor
New Zion Chapel First Baptist Church - Los Angeles
California

~~~~~~~~~~~~~~~~~~~~~~~~~~~~~~

The woman that we call 'The First Lady of Gospel Theater' may soon be known as 'The 'First Lady of Gospel Novels'. Ms. Michelle is brilliant! Her **'never say quit'** work ethics have certainly spilled over into her latest project. This book, based on the play *Is That Man Your Husband,* is a scintillating piece of work that displays the courage of a woman who's willing to put it all on the line. An impetuous and enchanting display of artful rhetoric, Ms. Michelle, First Lady of Gospel Theater, has another hit on her hands.

T.J. Hemphill
Playwright, Author

~~~~~~~~~~~~~~~~~~~~~~~~~~~~~~

Ms. Michelle, your process of thought was beautifully moving as your work in chapter one DID BLESS ME. You were used of God to help me see the story of the woman at the well in a different light. What a revelation God gave you! I loved your commentary after each scripture reference and the content did make sense, for it flowed nicely into the next segment of scripture. Oh, that a husband would follow the perfect example of Jesus! Though we come short, HE'S an example worth pursuing after. Chapter one spoke to my heart as a husband and challenged me to mark the perfect man (JESUS) and consider adapting HIS WAYS in dealing with my beloved spouse. It shared with me in an intimate way MY RESPONSIBILITY to her and gave me the tools to carry out that responsibility. Now, Chapter 5 TOTALLY AWESOME! The subject matter was intense and addictive to the senses. It was impossible to stop reading once you got started good and I loved the way, you engaged the reader in the story, sharing piece by piece, ever so carefully, the fine details of the story which eventually climaxed to the MAJOR EVENT that changed your life as you knew it then. You innocently shared how easily it is to be DECEIVED by one's own thoughts when you don't earnestly seek God's direction in every move and step you make.....Mostly, you shared the IMPORTANCE of personally knowing God's Word and proper interpretation FOR YOURSELF. The scripture says.... Study to shew THYSELF APPROVED UNTO GOD... ect. I loved your sub-titles to each section of work and it showed your "brilliant interpretation" for each sub-title foreshadowed to the reader what was to come. Once again, you honestly spoke from your heart and it showed your **transparency**, for this kind of writing ALWAYS MINISTER to the life of those that dare to read it.....

God Bless you.

Minister Antonious Thigpen

Introduction
Is That Man ... Your Husband?

The contents of this book are intended to share profound experiences and illuminate dark places relating to the universal subject of relationship. Let us pray so that when you read, your heart will be prepared and you will have an open mind to fully understand and **not** misinterpret the subject matters of this book.

Prayer:
Lord, I thank You for the divine inspiration to write these words that you have placed in my heart and now on the pages of this book. As I share my story, I pray that you will bless the reader of this book according to your divine will and purpose. Make clear to those who read the words in the pages to follow, the intent and motivation in which they were written. Allow the contents of this book to be received in the same spirit of LOVE from which they were inspired and expounded. Encourage and inspire your beloved readers to understand the distinct and needed differences between relationships with men versus a relationship with God ... use the content of this manuscript to enhance the way we all view and commit in our relationships with You and with each other. In Jesus' name I pray

Amen.

There are times when we look back over our lives and begin to wonder why we go through certain things only to find out later that what we experienced was only to strengthen and prepare us for our purpose and mission in life. One songwriter said, "As I look back over my life, I can see how your love has guided me. Even though I've done wrong, you never left me alone, but you forgave me and you kept on blessing." The Word of God declares in (KJV) **Lamentations 3:21-23** *"This I recall to my mind, therefore I have hope. It is of the Lord's mercies that we are not consumed, because his compassions fail not. They are new every morning: great is thy faithfulness".* And so the songwriter sings, "I could never repay you Lord for what you've done for me, for how you loosed the shackles and you made me free, how you made a way out of no way, turned my darkness into day. You've been my joy in the time of sorry, hope for my tomorrow, peace in the time of storm, strength when I'm weak and worn. As I look back over my life, I can surely say, "The Lord has certainly been faithful".

Writing this book was not an easy task and as you read you will understand why. Please understand that I write with no bitterness and my mission is not to condemn anyone. Instead, I hope to defend God's plan for sound spiritual leadership and encourage both men and women to Love and enter relationships God's way according to His Divine plan. The title of this book is a question ... and when I was asked this question, who would have thought that it would become the title of a national hit gospel stage play, a musical soundtrack with inspirational love songs, the signature question on underwear that promote sanctity in the bedroom ... and now the book that tells all? Hmmm? I certainly didn't. But praise God for witty inventions and for creativity. In this intriguing composition I tell the untold story behind the scenes and the laughter of the play. Intimately and openly sharing highlights of my life's journey and explaining step by step how I over came these challenges.

Chapter 1
The Thirst Quencher

Is That Man Your Husband? This question caused me to scratch my head in wonder when a special friend posed that question to me during a phone conversation in 1998. As we continued our conversation and read through the scriptural text noted in the fourth chapter of the book of St. John with our focus on verses 16,17 & 18, *(Old King James Version)* little did I know that the content of this conversation would be a pivotal point to redirect my life. And the question asked during this conversation would become the key that unlocked the vault to my destiny as a writer.

In these verses of scripture found in St. John chapter 4: 16-18, *(Old King James Version);* we find the biblical story of the woman of Samaria who met Jesus at Jacobs Well. During her conversation with Jesus, he told her to go and call her husband and come back to the well. She answered Jesus saying, "I have no husband", Jesus then replied saying, "You have well said I have no husband, you have had five husbands and the one that you are with now is **not** your husband."

Now, after my friend and I concluded our conversation, I continued to peruse through this scriptural community of the Bible and as I read, I wondered what was so significant about the woman going to the well at the noonday hour? Was it because she was thirsty? Hmmm? Yes of course, she was thirsty. But I believe her visit to the well at that particular hour was not just because she was thirsty but because she was destined to meet Jesus. Jesus, the only man who could quench her thirst, the man who could tell her all things, and minister to her very soul, the man who could speak life into her inward well and cause it to spring up into everlasting life.

I also wondered, "Why would a married woman tell a strange man that she'd just met at the well that she had no husband?" While in my moment of wonder, it was then that I realized that during my ten year marriage there had been many times that I had met strange men and wanted to tell them that I had no husband. Hmmm? Was it because I was not happily married? Was it because I had just had a disagreement with my spouse or was it simply because I was married to a Man ... but not my Husband? I suddenly began to think on my first encounter with Jesus, and although I had not known Him before, I was certainly known of Him, He knew all about me and He was no stranger at all. When he embraced me, my heart melted and I knew deep down in my soul that he would be the one man that would love me and never leave me. So when I think of the woman of Samaria meeting Jesus at the well, I wonder if her encounter with him was anything like mine. If it was, she had to be taken by his awesome presence and wooed by his marvelous words, because unlike any other man that I have ever dealt with, Jesus spoke words that gave life and inspired me to witness to others, even as the woman of Samaria did after meeting him.

(KJV) St John 4: 28, 29
"The woman left her water pot, and went her way into the city, and saith to the men. Come see a man, which told me all things that I ever did... Is not this the Christ?"

In other words, I believe she was saying, to the other men of the city... *"So you call yourself a man...*

*well all of you need to come see a real man that
knows how to pour and speak life into the spirit of
a woman quenching the very source of her thirst,
Is He not the epitome of a Husband?"* I believe
that this is one of the many biblical examples of
the effect that a husband's words should and will
have in the life of his wife.

Please understand that A MAN has dominion
and authority because God gave it to him ...

(KJV) GENESIS 1:26
*"And God said let us make man in our image,
after our likeness, and let them have dominion
over the fish of the sea, and over the fowl of the
air, and over the cattle and over all the earth,
and over every creeping thing that creepeth
upon the earth"*

But a HUSBAND has the divine nature of God,
housing the ability and the authority to love without
boundaries, like Hosea loved Gomer and YES ...
even as Christ loved the church and gave himself
for it.

(KJV) EPHESIANS 5:25
*"Husbands, love your wives, even as Christ also
loved the church, and gave himself for it..."*

Many times women and men alike, thirst for
love searching in all the wrong places, it's like
drinking soda or a milk shake to quench a thirst
that only water can diminish. The results of this kind
of thirst are devastating when a woman or a man
repeatedly open themselves up to receive what
is believed to be or portrayed as true love, only
to find out once again that it was not the real
thing. Oh how it hurts! Oh the pain! After going

through this kind of devastation one can become callused, and develop this mindset *"I will never be hurt like this again"*. They eventually refuse to live to love and would rather be bitter risking the chance of missing out on true love, rather than take the chance to deal with being hurt again. My question is, "What is life without love?" My advice is, "Don't allow some undeserving person to forfeit your destiny to love or to be loved, because "when a person can walk away from you or walk out of your life, let them walk" <u>T.D. JAKES</u>, it will work out for your good.

It is apparent that the woman of Samaria had more than a natural thirst for water and Jesus knew it, so he exercised his infinite wisdom and spoke direct to the source of her thirst saying,

St John 4:16
"...Go call thy husband and come hither"

When she answered and said,

St John 4:17
"...I have no husband"

Her response exposed her thirst. You see if we continue to drink soda and milk shakes when we are thirsty for water, after we have filled our bellies we will find that we are still thirsting, because the water is mixed with all kinds of artificial flavoring, sweeteners and other substances; which hinder the full effect of the water making the thirst greater than it was before. Well the woman that met Jesus at the well had a thirst for love, as do many of us ... this is why she had been with so many different men, and she was still thirsty. Like soda and milkshakes, she had dealt with men of different flavors who all had different sweeteners or (conversations) and substances or (personalities) but not one who could quench her real thirst.

(KJV) St. John 4:18
"For thou hast had five husbands and he whom thou now hast is not thy husband…"

Apparently none of them were equipped to love her the way she so deserved and desired this is why she was so thirsty and after hearing Jesus speak these profound words …

(KJV) St. John 4:14
"…Whosoever drinketh of the water that I shall give him shall never thirst, but the water that I shall give him shall be in him a well of water springing up into everlasting life."

When the woman heard this, she replied saying,

(KJV) St. John 4:15
"Sir, give me this water, that I thirst not, neither come hither to draw"

If you will allow me to interpret this portion of the conversation in my own words, I would say that Jesus was saying …
"My Beloved Queen, looky here, I can love you like no other, and if you would just give me a chance, I will never break your heart, I'll give you what you've been thirsting for because I am the thirst quencher, and you will never ever, ever, ever, thirst again"
And after she heard those words, she said,

"Alrighty then Boo, Show me what you working with, and if you doin' it like that, I won't be coming back here to draw water no more, and I will forever praise your name, it will be all about you." (smiling)

Although I have been hurt many times in my life and yes my heart has been broken a few times, I can't give up and I won't give in. I shall live and not die because Jesus has given me the authority to love and therefore I choose to live and to love. You see if I don't live, I can't love and if I don't love I risk a chance of living a miserable life. Please understand that love doesn't have to be shared with a bed partner if we simply learn to truly love ourselves. One of the reasons why we have trouble loving ourselves is because we think SEX has something to do with the foundation of love. Not true, and therefore life without love is miserable. God is Love and life without Him can be quite miserable.

(KJV) I John 4:7-8
7Beloved, let us love one another: for love is of God; and every one that loveth is born of God, and knoweth God.8He that loveth not knoweth not God; for God is love.

Because I know God, I choose to be better and not bitter and I understand that "rejection is direction." NOEL JONES

(KJV) Hebrews 10: 35, 36
35Cast not away therefore your confidence, which hath great recompence of reward. 36For ye have need of patience, that, after ye have done the will of God, ye might receive the promise.

There are times when I've longed for the opportunity to become one with my Husband, and there have been times when the enemy has tried to disguise longing as loneliness. Nevertheless I am not deceived and I am not ignorant of Satan's devices. I know and understand the difference between longing and loneliness. Longing simply means I have a desire, while loneliness is simply being alone and neither one is a bad thing. To desire or long for something purposeful is good because it acts as an emotional fuel that drives you into your destined place. And being alone is also good because it provides time for focus and instruction from your creator without distractions; which is required to get there, wherever your there is.

- Remember

Romans 8:28 (KJV)
28And we know that all things work together for good to them that love God, to them who are the called according to his purpose.

I believe and understand that a Husband is the only man besides Christ who is empowered to exercise his authority to love and provide with a commitment and without boundaries. He will speak life into the inward well of his wife and protect her. Therefore, a Husband is the one and only man worth waiting patiently for.

James 1:4 (KJV)
*... **Let patience have her perfect work**, that ye may be perfect and entire, wanting nothing.*

In the mean time Sister, be like Ruth and glean in the field, pursue your dreams, accomplish your goals. Stay fixed, focused and faithful, so that you can be fruitful. Your BOAZ will find you.

Ruth 2:3 (KJV)
³And she went, and came, and gleaned in the field after the reapers: ...

Ruth 2:5 (KJV)
... ⁵Then said Boaz unto his servant that was set over the reapers, Whose damsel is this?

Ruth 4:13(KJV)
¹³So Boaz took Ruth, and she was his wife: and when he went in unto her, the LORD gave her conception, and she bare a son.

Chapter 2
Tribulation or Preparation?

Someone asked me a question "Why did you marry the man that you married?" This person couldn't figure out how we ended up together, after knowing both of us for many years. This individual wanted to know what the attraction was between the man I married and myself, because it was apparent that we were diametrically opposed. Now, although it was not this persons business, for some odd reason I wanted to share just how I ended up married to this man. I shared with the individual that I allowed my church leader, the Apostle, to choose the man I married. Furthermore I stated that I had no attraction or desire to be involved with this young man that he chose. I married this man because I believed it would please the Apostle. Well, immediately this person asked me the same questions that are probably going though your mind right now. "Who is the Apostle?" "Why would you want to please him?" and "Why on earth would you allow him to choose your life partner? Hmm? Perhaps it was for the same reasons that other couples in the church allowed him to rule and break up their marriages. Shucks, if he could rule and break up other folks marriages, he could certainly put one together right? Needless to say, at that time I had no answer because the way I was taught, I thought it was the right thing to do. Sound ridiculous? Well, ten years later and after my divorce, I asked myself the same question. It was then I realized that although it was done indirectly, my partner and marriage was definitely the Apostle's choice but why did I allow the Apostle to choose my life partner? Well after asking the question, God began to make things clear as he opened my eyes.

James 1:5 (KJV)
*If any of you **lack wisdom**, let him ask of God, that giveth to all men liberally, and upbraideth not; and it shall be given him.*

As you read this next chapter, prayerfully you will understand, as I carefully explain in detail how and why I allowed the Apostle to choose my companion. And you will also be enlightened and made aware of the necessary boundaries that distinguish the difference between corrupt leadership and sound spiritual leadership.

Beware of the *(Cult)* disguised as *(Church)*
Cults - *A deceiving system of religious worship and ceremonies, designed and enforced by the leader in that particular house of worship, which causes it's follower's to have a twisted view of leadership, honoring them as God.*

Allow me to begin here ... In times past there have been a few cults that grew to numbers unimaginable such as the destructive doomsday cults, lead by *James Warren (Jim) Jones of (Jonestown, Guyana) & David Koresh of (Waco Texas)* to name a few.

Now, I know you are probably thinking what does *cults* have to do with the title of this book, I thought this book was about relationships and marriage, after all the title is

"Is That Man ...Your Husband?

Yes, you are absolutely right ... this book is about relationships and marriage but lets explore why someone would allow a Spiritual Leader/Pastor/

Apostle/Bishop etc... to have such authority in their life.

I want to talk to you about cultic behavior in the church that is not quite so easy to identify these days, because of the subtle approach and the route taken through the Word of God.

The type of cultic behavior that I personally experienced took place in churches that professed Christianity but had their own private interpretation of the bible. These types of congregations are commonly spear headed by leaders who operate in an outward position of power but secretly live in fear of what they don't know. This secret fear is generally disguised with open claims of having a special or exclusive position in ministry with gifts, revelation and a position of authority given to them by God, unlike any other. Also and most importantly, it is repeatedly and continuously brought to the attention of the followers how they must be obedient to the leader, however the leader has no accountability to anyone but his or her god; which in most cases, their gods are really a personal philosophy of how they see God.

I understand that the content in this chapter is very controversial, and in times past when I've confronted these issues, many who suffered the same spiritual abuse that I did have chosen to turn a deaf ear and look the other way. Because of that fact, I have dealt with the subject matter very delicately yet directly. My prayer is that you will read with an open heart and mind, and that God will give you understanding as I carefully share my story.

Please understand that I do **not** believe that all churches are operating as cults with teachings that deceptively rule the lives and the finances of the people, ultimately keeping them in bondage.

But rather I believe and know for certain that there are many that preach and teach the death, burial and resurrection of Jesus Christ our Lord and Savior according to biblical principals found in the Word of God. Furthermore I believe and know of churches that grow and become progressive ministries, filled with thankful people who have experienced seemingly impossible victories, live prosperous and fruitful lives, while sharing joyful life changing testimonies of how they have overcome. I am proud to say that I currently fellowship and serve under the auspices of a man of God who is the overseer of a progressive, fruitful ministry for which I am grateful because these days churches that care, help and restore lives are hard to find.

The leaders of these types of organizations disguised as church, hide the truth in the truth as they see it, causing the people who ignorantly follow, to harbor the hidden belief that their group or congregation is the only one with the whole truth and nothing but the truth; thereby provoking the followers to stand in strong defense for what they believe to be true. This belief then is based on what they have seen, heard and been taught exclusively by their spiritual leader. These groups operate with cultic mannerisms and must be exposed because it is ludicrous to believe that one person has all of the answers.

I want to believe that in these types of church groups, the leaders actually began with a sincere heart, believing that God had called them to ministry and given them a divine assignment to lead a flock of people to Christ. However, no matter how great my desire is to believe that these leaders had a sincere heart from the beginning, I am unable to digest that idea because it is written

...

I John 2:19 (KJV)
*"... They went out from us, but they were not
of us, for if they had been of us, they would no
doubt have continued with us; but they went
out that they might be made manifest that they
were not all of us."*

In other words, if you plant orange seeds you
get oranges, if you plant apple seeds you get
apples, right? Well if God plants a seed in a mans
heart to preach the Gospel of Jesus Christ, he will
preach the Gospel of Jesus Christ, and the fruit of
the Spirit of God will be made manifest in the lives
of the people who hear.

Colossians 1: 5, 6 (KJV)
*[5]..., whereof ye heard before in the word of the
truth of the gospel;*

*[6]Which is come unto you, as it is in all the world;
and bringeth forth fruit, as it doth also in you,
since the day ye heard of it, and knew the grace
of God in truth:*

Corrupt leaders are apparently self-made and
easily deceived by their own minds. I use to say,
"They *went* but they were not *sent*". This is true in
most cases because these prototypes were never
able to effectively nor submissively follow and
serve under the auspices of anyone else, however
they possess a strong, persuasive tongue filled with
reason of why they themselves should be followed.
You see good spiritual leaders are simply faithful
followers who end up out front, like Joshua after
the death of Moses; in fact Joshua became such
a great leader that his faithfulness as a follower

was recorded in the book of Deuteronomy and his succession as a leader in the book of Joshua.

Anyhow in these cultic type groups that we refer to as the church, the self-made leaders lose sight on God, misinterpret Christ-like authority and then act as God to the faithful people who have been persuaded that this person is following the ways of God, therefore they will follow. It is deception in one of its purist forms, because the people who faithfully follow have actually experienced some powerful life changing victories that their leaders were instrumental in helping them to get through; and as a result they are sub-conscienceless forced to believe that this person actually has the key or rather the connection with God that they themselves lack, therefore it breeds trust and dependence. As a result the followers are made to believe that there is an obvious need in their individual lives that can only be achieved through obeying their leaders every word.

I remember a time during my first few years in this particular church when the Apostle told us that we needed to live a holy life like him. He often said *"The Devil respects me"* and he really believed that lie because he went so far as to pass out pictures of himself to the congregation, telling us that if we found ourselves in a battle with the Devil or if we needed God to do something miraculous for us; all we would have to do is pull his picture out of our purses or wallets and lay our hands on the picture and say *"Apostle said, or the man of God said"* this or that. And in the name of Jesus it would come to pass. Now you **do** know that if Satan had no respect for God, why on earth would anyone believe that the devil would have any respect for flesh and blood?

The Apostle would base his statement on this particular scripture found in the book of Acts

Acts 19:15 (KJ V)
15And the evil spirit answered and said, Jesus I know, and Paul I know; but who are ye?

He would imply that he walked in the same authority and power that Apostle Paul walked in and therefore if the devil or evil spirits knew and respected Paul, then certainly the devil knew him too. Well there is no doubt in my mind that the devil knew him, however there is pertinent reason for me to doubt that the devil had the same level of respect for him as Paul or Jesus.

If we were to explore the text and look into the relevant details, we find that the Jewish exorcists were disgraced and their disorderly powerless actions were exposed. Some of the Ephesians even burned their evil books after hearing the word of God preached by the Apostle Paul. He was respected because his life apparently reflected his teachings and signs followed. In this scripture it is **not** Paul himself proclaiming that the devil knew who he was, it is in fact his life and works that prompted others to speak on his behalf as the evil spirit declares; *"Jesus I know and Paul I know, but who are ye?"* This reveals that an uncommon level of respect is indeed possible to obtain among principalities in high places, but only through Jesus Christ.

Now having said all of that, it was apparent that I very gullible because I faithfully followed the Apostle's teachings. I obeyed and trusted him with my life and so I did it. Yes, I would actually pull his picture out of my purse whenever I was dealing with something and I would tell the devil what the man of God said, with the expectation that whatever my request was would come to pass. How special is that!?

I was spiritually handicapped and dependant on this man as if he were my God or my only link or connection to God. When he would minister, it was like he put himself in Jesus' position, as if he had the power to change situations that Jesus died for, the kind of situations that only the true and living God could handle. Wow...that's scary isn't it... but what is even worse is that I believed him. In fact there was a time that I believed everything he said, even if I knew in my heart that what he said was wrong and made absolutely no sense according to the Word of God. Somehow I would manage to rationalize whatever he said and force it to make sense, because he couldn't be wrong, right? After all he was the Apostle. Was it some slick way to keep our minds on HIM when we were blessed, lonely, etc...? Hmm? Think about it?

(KJV) Matthew 15:14
...And if the blind lead the blind, both shall fall into the ditch.

I know from experience that when a person is persuaded to open themselves up and trust another person, with the kind of trust that is reserved for God, they become dependant, handicapped and crippled in their mind, ultimately relying on or placing confidence in that person, permitting them to speak into their lives with out fear or misgiving. When this occurs, deception is then blotted out even as an option. No one could tell you that this person is hurting you or will hurt you and/or lead you astray; and even if they did, you wouldn't believe it anyway. Why would you believe something so cruel about a person who is not only your spiritual leader but, this person is your friend, your confidant, your counselor, your parent and they've always expressed sincerity and concern in the image of Christ-likeness? Many of them actually speak positively from the Holy Bible quoting scripture while you experience life-changing miracles. You see, God can't lie and so in actuality these miracles that you have experienced happened based on your actual faith because **you** believed what the Word of God says, **not** because the leader told God what to do about your situation.

For example, I will share a circumstance that appeared at the time of occurrence to be one devastating tribulation. I went through this ordeal in early 1988 and this was one of many situations that the Apostle under whom I sat for some 10 years alleged glory for, after **God** delivered me out of the situation. Please understand that under no uncertain terms, my deliverance came from God, and so ... to God be the glory.

Now having said all of that, let's examine my situation and determine whether it was **tribulation or preparation**? Now, if your think tank is fueled by a positive outlook on life, and you understand what the word says when it states that "...all things work together for good to them that love God, to them who are the called according to his purpose" Romans 8:28; then you will clearly see that my situation was definitely preparation. However, if negativity is the fuel of your influence, then tribulation will be your obvious choice.

You see, I was in trouble with the law and facing 5 years in prison, because during the time that I was employed by a prominent department store, I gave clothes away, lots of clothes! When my discrepancy was discovered, I was charged with a felony, Grand Theft. I was devastated because this situation altered my promising future. And yes, my future was promising, that is if the future could be determined by prior events. Fortunately the future is not and can not be determined by the past or passed events.

Galatians 5:9 – 1 Corinthians 5:6
"...A little leaven, leaveneth the whole lump"

Although I had quite a *lump* of great things going on in my life, this seemingly unfortunate situation with the law was the little leaven that leaveneth my whole lump. In other words it was the monkey wrench that screwed up my plans. *Winner of an American Business Woman Scholarship 1986; Winner in the Miss Black Los Angeles Scholarship Beauty Pageant1988; Associate of Arts Degree in Fashion Merchandising and Marketing 1989; High profile fashion model, single, young, beautiful, vibrant and educated.* I was living on my own, and in pursuit of my dreams. Sound promising? Sure it does.

Well, when I managed to get myself caught up with the wrong people, I lost focus, and my level of integrity began to rapidly decline. As a result I began to decrease in my level of thinking which caused me to ignorantly give away merchandise that did not belong to me. Ultimately, it was stealing and when my inconsistency was revealed, I was faced with the right kind of trouble that caused me to run to Jesus, like the best of us do in similar situations.

While I was sitting in the holding tank of the county jail, I was discombobulated and I didn't know what to do but I had a male friend that I'd known since my teenaged years who had become a minister. Although I had not given a second thought to calling him before, his name was the only one I could think of during my visit to the county jail. You see, he had been witnessing to me about the love of Jesus Christ and diligently trying to get me to come to his church and hear his spiritual leader, the Apostle. Needless to say, he was unsuccessful in his quest until this trouble with the law came my way. He didn't have to call me or ask me to come to church anymore, this time I called him but I didn't call until after I got out of jail on bail.

God knew that this was the kind of trouble it would take to get my attention because I was living a glamorous life and coveted by many, but there was nothing glamorous or covetous about this state of affairs. So I called and wanted to come to church because I was scared and needed some supernatural help, the kind of help that could produce results that my beauty and booty couldn't achieve this time.

After a few weeks of attending his church, I finally found the courage to tell the Apostle and the other ministers in the church what I was going through; the little church family bonded together like glue and prayed with me through this faith-challenging situation. Hallelujah! The Apostle and the ministers accompanied me to court, through the entire trial process for a full year and ministered to me continuously. I received strength and encouragement daily spending most of my time at the church. Also during that pivotal year I received the baptism of the Holy Ghost in Jesus' name ... praise God, my life had been changed.

Not only did my life change during that year, but also my last name... yes, I got married in the midst of all of this drama, can you believe it? What was I thinking about? Well, I know you are probably thinking why would she marry during this uncertain period in her life?

Well after years of growth and change, I was thinking the same thing, so when I asked myself the same question, it was then that I realized I didn't need or want to be married at that time. The Apostle had suggested that I needed to be married in order to escape burning. Now even though I had no idea what he meant at the time he made that statement, I wanted to please the Apostle, because if it pleased the Apostle, it was like pleasing God, right? Wrong. I know, you are probably thinking why would anyone think that if they pleased the Pastor/Apostle/Bishop/Spiritual Leader etc., it would be like pleasing God? Well, that's how we were taught and furthermore, all of the members of this tiny congregation understood clearly that the sure way to please the Apostle was to be obedient not only to his direct instructions but also to his suggestions. So when he mentioned that I needed to be married it was only a matter of time. And honestly speaking I was also in need of comfort, compassion or simply a way to soothe the trouble that I was going through, as if marriage could help my situation. Boy! Was I naïve or what? I thought marriage would help my personal image look better in the eyes of the judge, because the truth was, I just wanted to get out of trouble with the law, I wasn't thinking about being married. I needed to be comforted, and I wanted to feel protected because I was dealing with a lot of stress; and what better way to achieve those things than to be married right? Wrong, really wrong. It was then that I was presented with an opportunity to learn to lean and depend on Jesus and have faith in God. However I was not being taught how to lean and depend on God but rather how to lean and depend on man. This is why I married in the midst of all of this drama. Understand now?

At any rate, the man that I married was not a bad person in fact he was a very nice young man with a warm heart. The problem is that love had nothing to do with our union. I wasn't in love when we were first married, in fact I didn't have time to even get to know him. You see, we met at a Harvest Musical on Halloween weekend October 1989 and married 3 weeks later before the Thanksgiving holiday, it all happened so fast. I thought at some point I would learn to love him or grow to love this man who was so willing to marry me, even though he knew I was on my way to prison. Isn't that what every one wants? To be loved in spite of our short comings? Think about it, his willingness to marry me in the midst of all of the drama that was going on in my life was rather noble of him don't you think? Well I thought so too, but I soon learned that it was not a noble act at all, it was pure ignorance charged by the lustful fire that filled his pants. After we were married, it became apparent that he just wanted to be married so he could have sanctified sex and I just wanted to be married to improve my image to the judge hoping to get out of trouble and be comforted in my flesh. And furthermore, he would have married anyone that was willing to say yes, I was willing.

We were both two very misguided young people looking for love in the wrong places. And the Apostle was so wrong for encouraging and even partaking in such a union. There was no real pre-marital counsel administered because there was no qualified counselor in our presence. No not even the Apostle, even though he had been married a few times and carried the biblical title *"Apostle"*. When I asked the Apostle about premarital counsel, and after he pulled a white handkerchief out of his pocket for an illustration piece, he said *"This is the boy you need to marry because he is like this white handkerchief, he is clean"*. Honestly I didn't know what that meant but I guess it sounded alright to me at the time because I received what the Apostle said, I began to thank the Lord for a young *clean* man and a week later we were married. Now remember I was still going through those court hearings and so my young clean husband soon became one of the ministers who accompanied me to court for the rest of that trying year.

Finally, after a year of going through court hearings, I was sentenced to 3 years in prison, 2 years probation and $15,000 in restitution payments. Oh my God! I was devastated, where was God? For crying out loud, I had never been in any trouble before and that was a pretty harsh judgment don't you agree? I didn't know what to think, my little heart was crushed. It seemed that just a few days ago I was walking across a stage receiving honors at graduation with a promising future and then all of a sudden I was standing in front of a judge facing prison time. All of this just didn't make sense. How in the world did I end up here? In my heart I was hoping that God would do something big like cause an earthquake or something just to let the judge know that He was on my side but there was no sign of anything like that about to take place. But then, while in court, the Apostle told me to plead with the judge, so I did. I opened my mouth and said, **"Please have mercy Judge, Jesus has changed my mind and my ways, and He has given me a new life, I am not the same person anymore".** Can you believe the judge thought I was crazy? And in addition to what he had already stated, he also ordered me to seek psychiatric help...? Yes... I said psychiatric help. After the judge stated his thoughts, the Apostle stood up in my defense and pleaded my case, saying, "*Judge this is her first offence*" yet still, the judge wouldn't budge. But I must say the Apostle's efforts were admirable. However in the end, despite the sentence that I was given, God, the judge of mankind, had mercy. Here is the miracle working power of God, *I only served 30 days in prison, paid $500 in restitution, did some community service at a local recreation center, got my record sealed and the only thing close to psychiatric help that I received was the sermons that I heard in the church where I fellowshipped.* God had worked a miracle and answered my prayers, according to I Corinthians 10:13, I prayed Lord forgive me for allowing temptation to overtake me and for the wrong that I have done and Lord thank you for making a way of escape, not putting more on me than I could bear. And then I praised God for his goodness and His mercy.

1 Corinthians 10:13 (King James Version)
¹³There hath no temptation taken you but such as is common to man: but God is faithful, who will not suffer you to be tempted above that ye are able; but will with the temptation also make a way to escape, that ye may be able to bear it.

Chapter 3
Three Days

According to the Holy Bible many notable miracles took place within three days.

Within _three days_ Joshua and the Children of Israel crossed the Jordan River and took Possession of the Promised Land.

Joshua 1:11
Pass through the host, and command the people, saying, Prepare you victuals; for within three days ye shall pass over this Jordan, to go in to possess the land, which the LORD your God giveth you to possess it.

A decree to kill all of Esther's kindred was sent out, but after _three days_ of fasting their lives were spared.

Esther 4:16
*Go, gather together all the Jews that are present in Shushan, and fast ye for me, and neither eat nor drink **three days**, night or day: I also and my maidens will fast likewise; and so will I go in unto the king, which is not according to the law: and if I perish, I perish.*

Jonah was instructed to go and preach to the people of Nineveh, but he decided to go on a cruise instead, he was tossed over board, swallowed by a great fish and lodged there in the belly of the fish for _three days_ and three nights.

Jonah 1:17
*Now the LORD had prepared a great fish to swallow up Jonah. And Jonah was in the belly of the fish **three days** and **three** nights.*

Jonah 3:3
*So Jonah arose, and went unto Nineveh, according to the word of the LORD. Now Nineveh was an exceeding great city of **three days**' journey.*

Jonah ended up right back where the Lord instructed him to go in the first place and then a Great Deliverance Ministry was birthed. Imagine the multitudes that will be blessed by your life when you line up with the will of God.

Jonah was an example of the Deliverance Ministry that was yet to come through Jesus Christ for the World.

Matthew 12:40
*For as Jonas was **three days** and **three** nights in the whale's belly; so shall the Son of man be **three days** and **three** nights in the heart of the earth.*

If Death couldn't hold Jesus down in the grave, what makes you think that anything can hold you down in the earth, if the Spirit of Him who God raised up from the dead be in you?

John 2:19
*Jesus answered and said unto them, Destroy this temple, and in **three days** I will raise it up.*

He said it and it came to pass. Life and death are in the power of your own tongue, speak life and it will come to pass.

Proverbs 18:21
Death and **life** are in the **power** of the **tongue**: and they that love it shall eat the fruit thereof.

"My Three Day Miracle"

I would like to share one of the **three day** miracles that manifested in my life during my 30 day visit to prison. This is one miracle that I will never forget. I had been in prison for 27 days, humbly serving my three year sentence. I was sitting in the prison yard on one of the benches, minding my own business. I was reading my bible when a small group of other inmates who were apparently **very** familiar with prison life walked up to harass me. The leader of the pack stepped up behind me and shoved the back of my head into my bible and said, **"You know every body wants to get holy when they come to prison, but that bible can't protect you in here, this is my territory and I'm gone make you my B****."**

Now, even though I wanted to hit her up-side her head with my bible after she shoved the back of my head, I didn't. Honestly I was a little bit scared, No... I was petrified, because I didn't know what was about to go down. All I had to depend on for protection was my faith in the content of the little black bible that I was holding firmly in my hands. So what was I supposed to do? Should I have hit her up-side her head with my bible? Of course not, that would have been ignorant because first of all it was more than one of them and when you get in trouble on the inside, it could lead to more prison time. Not to mention it would not have been very Christian like. So I praise God for wisdom and for allowing this to be a golden opportunity for me to see His Word manifested as my divine protection. But, I couldn't just sit there and let her bully me I had to say something. And so I said, as nicely as I possibly could, *"I was holy before I came to prison"* She quickly responded as she rolled her neck, putting one hand on her hip and the other in my face saying, *"If you were holy before you got here you wouldn't be here"* leaning back I said, *"No, that's not true, the truth is I wasn't holy when I did what put me here, but I was definitely holy before I came here"* She then slowly walked away with her posse saying, *"Yeah whatever"* shaking her head like I was crazy or something then looking back at me with a *sarcastic evil grin* on her face silently mouthing the words **"I'm gone get you."** Was I nervous? Was I scared? Yes of course, I was nervous and shaken, but deep down in my soul I was confident that God would take care of me. Then before I knew it... I stood up and said with a loud voice, *"I will be out of here in <u>three days.</u>"* What in the world was I talking about, I had been sentenced to serve three years, and I had only been there for 27 days. I must have appeared as if I were a little touched (if you know what I mean) because news travels fast in prison and they knew that I was sentenced to serve three years. They all laughed at me and began to mock me, because they had already got the scoop on me. Not only did they know my sentence time, but they knew my name and why I was there. I sat down nervously shaken in my spirit trying to figure out why I had just stood up and boldly spoke with a loud voice and a little bit of attitude **"I will be out of here in <u>three days</u>"** I couldn't figure it out, so I opened my bible and tried to continue reading but I couldn't get focused because I was nervous and scared and looking continuously over my shoulders thinking they would come back. Nonetheless, soon the time came for lock down or bedtime, but I couldn't sleep because I couldn't get those words that I had spoken, out of my head. So I prayed to God asking for understanding and then I opened my bible and began to read. I was up almost all night searching the scriptures for comfort before I finally fell asleep. While I searched the scriptures, I remember coming across this passage in

I Corinthians 10:13
Where it says ...

1 Corinthians 10:13 (KJ V)
[13]There hath no temptation taken you but such as is common to man: but God is faithful, who will not suffer you to be tempted above that ye are able; but will with the temptation also make a way to escape, that ye may be able to bear it.

After reading this scripture, I asked God to forgive me and make a way of escape from this unfortunate prison situation because three years in prison was more than I could bear. I had also read about how the angel of the Lord came and freed Peter from prison...

Acts 12:7 **(KJV)**
*And, behold, the angel of the Lord came upon him, and a light shined in the **prison**: and he smote **Peter** on the side, and raised him up, saying, Arise up quickly. And his chains fell off from his hands.*

...And I believed God for my miracle even though I couldn't see it, I believed by faith.

Hebrews 11:1 **(KJV)**
Now faith *is the* **substance** *of things hoped for, the evidence of things not seen*

Well, the next morning quickly came and the words that I had spoken were still ringing in my head. **"I will be out of here in three days."** The jailers came in calling for the inmates to line up for breakfast or morning chow as it is referred to (in prison), and while I was eating breakfast I saw the pack of inmates that harassed me the day before. They were looking at me and talking among themselves. My heart began beating fast and hard. Fear gripped my heart and I began to imagine horrible things like being gang raped. As my heart continued to pound and sweat began to release under my arms, in the palm of my hands, and from my forehead, you would have thought I had just had a workout with the drum line of the band from Grambling State University. I couldn't wait to finish breakfast so I could get out of their eye sight and relax my nerves. You know, out of sight, out of mind. Anyway, I didn't know what they were plotting so I kept my face in my bible and I stayed clear of them for the next few days.

On the 30th day of my being locked up in prison, which was also the 3rd day after I spoke the profound words **"I will be out of here in <u>three days</u>."** I call these words profound because they soon proved to be very insightful after the manifestation of a miracle. Anyway, I was focused on God's word and there was no wavering in my faith, I believed that God would get me out. In my heart I felt like Shadrach, Meshach and Abednego, when they were in trouble with King Nebuchadnezzar because they wouldn't bow down and serve his god. They loved and trusted their God so much that even when they were faced with the threat of being thrown into the burning fiery furnace, they declared that even if God didn't deliver them out of the fiery furnace, they would not bow down and serve a golden image.

Daniel 3 (KJV)

[17]If it be so, our God whom we serve is able to deliver us from the burning fiery furnace, and he will deliver us out of thine hand, O king.

[18]But if not, be it known unto thee, O king that we will not serve thy gods, nor worship the golden image which thou hast set up.

After reading these passages of scripture found in the infallible Word of God, I was encouraged, inspired and my faith was certainly increased. I decided in my heart and made up in my mind that even if God didn't deliver me out of prison that day, I would love Him and serve Him just because He is God, and I would not become insecure in my faith. Furthermore I made up in my mind that I would share the Gospel of Jesus Christ and His love no matter where I ended up, because I was sold out to Him.

"THE RELEASE CALL"

Every day in prison there was a release call. In fact there were **three** release calls each day, one in the morning, one in the afternoon and one in the early evening. On that particular day, which was the third day, I arose with a great expectation in my spirit. So when the bell rang for the first release call, and the jailer began to speak over the intercom system announcing the names and numbers of the inmates to be released that day, I sat on the edge of my bunk, praying and listening attentively for my name to be called. They did not call my name or my number in the first release call, but I was not giving up hope because there were two more release calls yet to come. The noon hour couldn't come fast enough and when the bell rang for the second release call, the jailer began to speak over the intercom, I sat on the edge of my bunk once again nervously clutching the rails of the bed, praying for Gods mercy, and again I didn't hear my name or my number. I began to feel a little bit shaken because the facts of the sentence that was given to me were running through my mind, with the clear intent to intimidate my faith. And the facts included a three-year prison sentence with a possibility for parole after eighteen months served. I had only been there for thirty days, so was I crazy to believe that God could change things through prayer and faith, or was I just foolish enough to believe that God could use my situation to confound the wisdom of men? Well, I will tell you, although I was shaken up a bit, my faith was untouched. I believed God for my miracle and I began to praise God for his unmatched love, for his mercy and for sending his only begotten son to die for me taking my place on the cross in the pardon of my sins. Finally the three o'clock hour came and it was time for the final release call. I sat confidently on the edge of my assigned bunk, with my ears sharply tuned in to listen for my name. I just knew that my name would be called even though the facts stated the contrary and in-spite of the sentence given, I believed God with every thing in me. All of the signs were there, my faith was in place and the word of God had declared that I could be free. So, I listened and listened with great expectation during the third a final release call as the jailer slowly and clearly called the names of the inmates that were being released. After the jailer called the final name on the list and after I realized that I did not hear my name called, I was in a serious state of devastation. I was discombobulated, breathless and overcome with defeat. For a brief moment I felt utterly abandoned. When I think back on that devastating moment, it is clear to me why Jesus spoke these words when he was hanging on the cross ...

<u>Psalm 22:1</u>
My God, my God, **why hast thou forsaken me**? **why** *art* **thou** *so far from helping* **me**, *and from the words of my roaring?*

<u>Matthew 27:46</u>
And about the ninth hour Jesus cried with a loud voice, saying, Eli, Eli, lama sabachthani? that is to say, My God, my God, **why hast thou forsaken me**?

Although Jesus knew his divine purpose, willingly fulfilled his mission on earth; yet and still, when the appointed time came and he was hanging on the cross, his flesh cried out because he felt abandoned just for a brief moment. Had God really forsaken him? No not at all.

<u>Hebrews 13:5</u>
Let your conversation be without covetousness; and be content with such things as ye have: for he hath said, I will **never leave thee, nor forsake thee**.

God will never leave nor forsake us. He did not forsake his only begotten son on the cross and He did not forsake me, even thou I felt abandoned in my flesh for that brief moment. I vividly remember dropping my head in shame because I did not hear my name called, but it was at that moment that I realized how much I really loved God, no matter what. I didn't love him only for what He could do for me I loved him just for being my God, for opening his heart to receive me just as I was. I was a felon, a convict, a liar, and a thief, but God received me and loved me anyway. After reflecting on these things, I became conscious of this one very important thing, and that one thing is that I had actually fallen in love with the spirit of God. I suddenly felt so much love for him that I was overcome with gratefulness. I then opened my mouth and said, "Lord I still love you, trust you and I will praise you no matter what". Yes even if he didn't get me out of prison, because I believed that he knew what was best for me. Suddenly I heard the patter of feet rushing in my direction as I sat there on the edge of the bunk. I looked up and saw that is was the inmate who had harassed me a few days prior. I thought I was going to have to fight, because she was moving rapidly in my direction, and there were no jailers in sight. When she was within a few feet of my space, and I realized that she was indeed headed towards me, I jumped up to prepare for defense, but she swiftly passed right by me and quickly grabbed my blanket, rolled it up with my belongings, shoved it into my arms and told me that I'd better hurry up because they'd already called my name twice. I was standing there in a state of shock trying to figure out what was going on. What was she talking about? And then suddenly the jailer's voice came back over the intercom and **for the third time**, called out the names of those inmates that were being released. It was then that I heard my name, **oh my God! Did you hear what I just said? I said,** "I heard my name!" Hallelujah! Praise Jesus! Isn't it ironic that I did **not** hear my name called the first two times **on the third release call** when I was the one attentively listening for my name? In fact, my name was being called for the **third time** when I actually heard it. However, the inmate who boldly told me that the bible couldn't help me in prison, yes, the same one who'd harassed me and shoved my head into my bible a few days before, the same one that I'd shouted the prophetic words to when I said **"I will be out of here in three days."** She was the one that God allowed to hear my name called before I heard it. Yes, she heard my name and that is why she ran over to my bunk and rolled up my belongings with tears in her eyes. She was coming to tell me that my name had been called. I suppose she had tears in her eyes because she knew that it had to be God, working this situation out in my favor, because I was sentenced to serve three years yet I was being released after only serving thirty days. Hallelujah, praise Jesus! Wow! It was then that I realized that my God is not only ALL powerful but He also has quite a sense of humor.

His actions stated loud and clear that not only can His holy Word help me while in prison but it can also make me free. As she handed me my belongings and gently shoved me towards the exit door, I looked back at her as she spoke these **three** very humbling words *"Pray for me"*.

I praise God for His goodness and for His mercy! I thank him for working a noted miracle in my life in **THREE DAYS!**

Chapter 4
Beware of Wolves in
Sheep's Clothing

After God had shown his mercy in bringing me safely through the state of affairs that I expounded upon in chapters two and three, I was grateful, thankful and humbled by His Grace; just as anyone with a conscience would be after going through an ordeal of that magnitude. This is why I've concluded that the after effects of the Apostle's actions were rather bizarre. Permit me to explain. You see, it appeared to me that his method and direction in ministry began to change from what seemed to be pure into something filled with mischief and deceit.

I've spent years reflecting on the Apostles teachings, and how his expressions affected my life. And the more I examined the flow of his delivery I discovered that his method of ministry exemplified the characteristics of a cult.

For illustration, allow me to share this very real scenario. I am sure we can agree that when ever God or anyone does something nice for someone else, an attitude of gratitude is expected to follow. Well in the state of affairs pertaining to my deliverance from the prison, instead of being grateful, thankful and humbled by God's mercy, the Apostle began to glorify and magnify my testimony by telling it more than I did. He would often and cleverly compare my testimony to his own. He had come out of quite a few things himself, including pimping women, drugs, gambling, almost losing his mind after being beat in the head with pool sticks and having a plastic plate placed in his head.

There were times when he would tell my testimony in such a way that I felt like a movie star. Sound ridiculous? I'm sure it does, but it is true. He would go to extreme measures to glorify what God had done for me and I had no problem with that because God deserved the Glory for what he had done. However, testimonies are given to uplift and set others free, not to condemn or make others feel inadequate.

Revelation 12:11

And they overcame him by the blood of the Lamb, and by the word of their testimony; *and they loved not their lives unto the death.*

It disturbed my spirit when the Apostle would give his dissertation of my testimony because his delivery constantly made others in the church feel like they had no testimony at all. For example if your life had simply taken a different route in getting to Jesus, one that was not as shady in comparison to his or mine you would feel like your testimony was not worth telling.

The Apostle would frequently imply the promotion of himself as a powerful leader by often making blatant and bold statements about other spiritual leaders whose ministries were in full bloom. He would conclude that the reason for other ministries growing so rapidly was because the leaders were homosexuals. Well, I conclude that the Apostle would have said anything to condemn others in his effort to commend himself.

He time and again used my testimony and the testimony of others as influence over the radio and through other mediums in his attempt to catapult his ministry to the level that he coveted. It was apparent that the Apostle had his own ministry building agenda. Those of us who had been persuaded that this one man had all the answers were so programmed that every time anyone of us shared our testimony, we made sure that we gave the Apostle his portion of glory.

Now please understand that I believe honor should be given to whom honor is due according to the word of God...

<u>Romans 13:7</u>
*Render therefore to all their dues: tribute to whom tribute is **due**; custom to whom custom; fear to whom fear; honour to whom honour.*

And yes indeed the Apostle was instrumental in helping many of us to get our break through, but something happened when the glory was misplaced.

MISPLACED GLORY

After looking back through clear eyes and with a restored spirit, I believe that the Apostle really sincerely believed that his method of ministry was setting the captives free, and that he was doing no harm to anyone, not even himself. However the truth is that he was simply controlling and manipulating anyone who was ignorant enough to allow this type of control or hegemony to take place in their life.

Interesting enough, in my ignorance, I endorsed his claims, his ministry method and anything else that he set forth to accomplish by agreeing with everything that he said and also by obeying his every word. I had so much confidence in this man that I would excel to the point of defending his character against anyone who had something derogatory to say. I was a die hard Apostle fan and in my eyes he could do no wrong. Now please understand that I think it's wonderful and admirable to have that level of respect and regard for our Pastors/Apostles/Bishops/Spiritual Leaders etc.

1 Timothy 5:18 (KJV)
[18]For the scripture saith, thou shalt not muzzle the ox that treadeth out the corn. And, The labourer is worthy of his reward.

However there has to be balance, and balance must be taught. God has given every man a measure of faith and if we listen attentively to the Lord with our hearts and have faith, we shall know the truth when we hear it. And the truth will make us free. I have learned to trust no man completely, not even myself.

If you will permit me to glean from my own personal experience I have found that the dangers of misplaced glory is not when God actually honors His Holy Word, blesses and changes life's situations, but rather it becomes dangerous when leaders step into the tempting yet destructive thought that causes one to believe that it was somehow his or her power and authority that caused the blessing to take place. Furthermore when this occurs it should become apparent that one has strayed away from the ways of God because the result is self-exaltation. This is the canal through which cultic behavior is birthed. Not only do these types of leaders believe that they are always correct and never wrong, but most dangerously the faithful few who follow believe also.

Now, when a person has been persuaded to believe and trust to this magnitude, like I did, they look to their leaders for approval of everything that they do, and lose the ability to make decisions on their own. I remember asking the Apostle ridiculously ignorant questions like, how often do you think I should make love to my husband and what kind of facial cleanser should I use? I know it sounds silly but it's real. I was afraid to do anything without his approval. Now I know you are saying to yourself, why on earth would anyone ask their Pastor how often they should make love to their husband or their wife? Well, I will tell you why.

First let me paint a picture for you. Imagine this, you get up at 4:00 am in the morning to catch a bus at 5:00 am so you can get your baby to the sitter and make it to work by 7:00 am. Your bus ride is approximately 2 ½ hours. You work Eight hours on the job, and then catch another bus to the baby sitters house to pick up your baby and then walk 3 city blocks to the church, so you can get there by 7:00 pm. You've not had time to go home relax and collect yourself, you just keep going, not because you are so in love with God, but because you want to show yourself to be faithful to your leader and you didn't want to be the featured topic in the sermon for the evening. You then sit through church service from 7:00 pm to 11:00 pm on a good night but most of the time you are there until after Midnight because the Apostle always had a lot to say. Imagine this is your routine 5 days a week, every week. **_Are you tired yet?_** Well I was. So imagine being tired after all of this activity and then sitting in service falling asleep while the Apostle was preaching one of his normal four hour sermons. He would openly rebuke or harshly chastise anyone who fell asleep during his Sermon. This Apostle would stand boldly in the pulpit and yell at us saying, things like this...

"Y'all is too young to be sleeping in the church, when I was ya'll age I had energy and now I'm 50 years old and still got more energy than ya'll got"

He would go on to say, *"I know what the problem is, **ya'll got bed ticks**"*

Now, the first time he shared that original phrase, I concluded that it was a rather creative use of terminology and I wasn't certain what he meant, but after sitting under his leadership for so long, I learned the lingo. I believed he was saying that we were having too much sex, and low and behold I was absolutely right. Before I could get the thought processed through my mind, he said

"Ya'll is having too much sex, and you can't praise God, cause you're in the flesh"

Well, even thou I knew that wasn't true, once again I managed to rationalize his theory and I simply agreed with him because it was always easier to agree with him rather than holding opposing views. In my heart I just wanted to line up with what I thought was the will of God. I didn't want to be named among them that were rebellious or disobedient. This is why I asked the Apostle **"How often he thought I should have make love with my husband?"** Now although the Apostle wasn't a very educated man, he was smart enough **not** to answer this type of question in private. But he gladly used the pulpit as a platform to layout a love making schedule for all of the married couples in the church during one of his lengthy and perplexing sermons. This would be the Sunday morning message...scary huh? Well how about this... In the pivotal year of 1998 I was asked the famous question **"Is That Man Your Husband?"** But if I were asked that very same question ten years **prior** in 1989, my reply would have been *"If Apostle says it is so, it is so"*.

FINE LINE BETWEEN Leading & Controlling

<u>2 Corinthians 3:17</u>
*Now the Lord **is** that Spirit: and where the Spirit of the Lord **is, there is liberty**.*

    Spiritually speaking, the Church is supposed to be a place where believers come together to worship and celebrate the Lord our God, a spiritual hospital for the sin sick soul, a place that is symbolic to having a full course meal and dessert with the savior, a safe haven for the believer, a place where God's word is expounded upon in an effort to impart, restore or increase our faith. However it appears that many congregations that come together all in the name of "church" are not exemplifying the body of Christ, which is the church. Many religious organizations operate as a small den for lions where the leaders complain about irrelevant things like the famous building fund. While on the other end of the hemisphere we find that our churches have become corporate commercial giants and media gurus in a new religious world where the leader is untouchable and unreachable. What does all of this mean? Does it mean that the church has lost its power? No not at all, that is absurd. You see, the body of Christ is the church and it was His blood that was shed for the remission of our sins and the blood will never ever lose its power. I would advise all to know God for yourself making sure that you have a relationship with your maker and not religion according to a man's system of belief. Religion according to a man could prove to be devastating. But be of good cheer because the word of God says...

44

Jeremiah 23

¹Woe be unto the pastors that destroy and scatter the sheep of my pasture! saith the LORD.

²Therefore thus saith the LORD God of Israel against the pastors that feed my people; Ye have scattered my flock, and driven them away, and have not visited them: behold, I will visit upon you the evil of your doings, saith the LORD.

³And I will gather the **remnant** *of my flock out of all countries whither I have driven them, and will bring them again to their folds; and they shall be fruitful and increase.*

ARE YOU THE REMNANT? ... I AM THE REMNANT

While I sat under the guidance of this man who called himself an Apostle, I felt like I was on lock down, I couldn't put my hand on it, but I remember feeling that way all the time. Once, early in my walk with Christ, I planned a little trip to go and visit my family in Las Vegas, which was something I'd always done, it was not something out of the norm for me. But, apparently my Leader, the Apostle had a problem with me going home to see my family because he expressed his dismay by saying, things like ...

"Daughter, you aint ready to go visit your family yet, they are not saved, and you aint strong enough to deal with people in the world with worldly minds."

I didn't understand his intent for making this statement especially since this was my immediate family that he was referring to, not some group of strangers.

Anyhow he went on with his dissertation, confusingly changing the subject to his opinion about my communication with men. You see, he always jumped around in his conversations and I found him really hard to understand most of the time, but I thought if I just went with the flow I would eventually understand him, like everyone else seemed to. I really didn't know what angle his conversation was coming from because the two subjects had nothing to do with each other. I certainly didn't realize how much his words were affecting me and I didn't really understand what he was trying to tell me at that time, so I ended up going to see my family anyway. After my trip I came back to a spiritual war zone that I had no idea even existed.

The Trip

I chose to take the bus because I was just coming out of college and couldn't afford an airline ticket. When I was at the bus station waiting to depart, I laid eyes on this young man who was boarding the same bus. And that's when the first sign of mind control began to surface in my life. Let me explain....

Mind Control – Misplaced Authority

I remember thoughts coming to my mind and I began thinking about some of the things that the Apostle had said about my communicating with men... and suddenly a fear came over me and I was afraid to even look at the young man. I had never been afraid of anything before, so it was clear that something had changed about me. I remember the Apostle saying ...

"If I looked at a man I would end up burning"

Well I was so young in the Lord that I thought he meant I would burn in Hell if I looked at a man or even communicated with a man that I wasn't married to. However, that couldn't have been what he was saying because if it were, how on earth would I ever meet my husband. Hmmm? I couldn't figure it out and I was afraid to ask for clarification.

Suddenly I began to feel unsafe, like I shouldn't even be going on this trip unless someone in a position of authority was coming with me, someone like the Apostle, to supervise my activities. But why was I thinking like this all of a sudden? What was going on in my mind to cause me to think I needed supervision or permission to interact with people? Was I not the same young lady that won an academic scholarship and prepared to take on the world and pursue my dreams with no fear? Did God save me to isolate me from the world or from unsaved people? No of course not, if that were the case then, that would have meant that I couldn't communicate with anyone in my family, because none of them at that time were professing Jesus Christ as Lord and Savior. And then God would be a liar because the bible says ...

Mark 16:15
And he said unto them, Go **ye into all** *the* **world,** *and preach the gospel to every creature.*

So what was I supposed to do? I was confused and I was already on my way. I boarded the bus, trying desperately to avoid any eye contact with the young man, but he was zany and bold and he knew that I was avoiding him. So he ended up sitting in the seat right next to me. Oh my God! I was scared to death, but why was I afraid? I believe it was because I felt an attraction to this young man, I didn't know how I should respond, and not to mention the words that came out of the Apostles mouth were flooding my thoughts, which ultimately altered my outgoing, free spirited personality.

Anyway, this young man ended up keeping me company, as we began our journey to our destinations, and boy could he talk! He shared his dreams and kept me laughing all the way to Barstow, California, which is where he was getting off, because he was going there to perform. We ended up exchanging numbers before he got off the bus and it was then that I realized, talking to him was refreshing, I actually liked him. Nevertheless I slept the rest of the way to Vegas and after arriving, I met with my family, all went well and I ended up enjoying my visit with my family to the utmost.

After the Trip

When I came back to California and went back to church I experienced a chastisement that literally felt like a physical beating. I felt like a kid who had stolen some candy from the local convenience store, who got caught and then beaten by the parent all the way back to the store, in front of everyone. Can you imagine the humiliation of an event like that? Well, that's how I felt when the Apostle stood in the pulpit arrayed in his glory preparing to go forth and preach his sermon. I opened my bible preparing to follow along as he called out the scriptures from which he would bring his message, which is the normal protocol. He then began his prolific dissertation, which turned out to be a spiritual beat down. Allow me to describe the situation.

For example most of his sermons would come forth in this manner. He would take a text from a scripture like the one noted here in the book of Hebrews and he would break it down like this.

Heb 13 and 7 says,

"Obey them which have the rule over you, who have spoken unto you the Word of God: whose faith follow, considering the end of there conversation."

He would speak with emphasis on the first part of that scripture, **"Obey them which have the rule over you..."**as he went forth, I felt like I was the only person in the church as he spoke indirectly about my trip. He used disobedience as a subject matter, and the fact that I'd went on the trip as the example to demonstrate and make his message plain to the congregation.

He began to teach and preach that if we, meaning all ten members of the church, did not want to obey him, then we could leave and find ourselves a new Leader. He also declared that he would not watch over the souls of disobedient children, who insist on doing what they want to do. He went on to say that there was no one else in town preaching the word like him, he told us often that most Leaders were homosexuals, and he implied that if we left, God would not be pleased and furthermore the only reason anyone has ever left his church is because they couldn't stand to hear the truth and they couldn't take instructions from the man of God.

He would then take another scripture like this one noted in the book of Ephesians to back up his explanation

Ephesians chapter 2:1-3

1) And you hath he quickened who were dead in trespasses and sins; 2) wherein in times past you walked according to the course of this world, according to the prince of the power of the

*air, the spirit that now worketh in the <u>children of</u>
<u>disobedience</u> 3) among whom also we all had
our conversation in times past in the lusts of our
flesh, and of the mind, and were by nature the
children of wrath even as others"*

After reading these verses of scripture, with his
emphasis on the **"children of disobedience"** he
would begin to explain his interpretation of the
text. However, his interpretations seemed to always
benefit him and somehow always painted a portrait
of him being a flawless leader. He stated that the
Devil is the prince and the power of the air, and
when a person is disobedient it is the Devil working
in them. He further explained, that we all have
lusts in our flesh that talk to us and entice us with
conversation from our past, but if we were really
filled with the Holy Ghost and if we really loved the
Lord, then we should have no problem obeying
our leader, understanding that obedience is better
than sacrifice.

He continuously told us stories about some of
the people who left his church in the past; making
examples of them, telling us how they lost their
minds, everything that they once had and how
they never prospered in anything. I submit that this
was his way of imparting fear in our hearts.

He would then close his message with yet even
more scriptures, like these noted in the book of
Ephesians that would confirm the message he was
aiming to get across.

Ephesians 6:1 and then also verses 5 - 7
*Verse 1 Children obey your parents in the Lord:
for this is right...*

He made it clear that he was our Parent in the Lord, and according to the word of God, it was just the right thing to do, obey him. He would go even further to explain that **verses 5-7** would help us to understand the attitude in which we should obey our leader ...

Verse 5)
Servants be obedient to them that are your masters according to the flesh, with fear and trembling in singleness of heart, as unto Christ.

In the Apostles words, he would say things like *"I am anointed and I am your master-builder like Apostle Paul, I am your Apostle and I am here in the flesh with you and if you can't obey me, how can you obey God?"*

Verse 6)
Not with eye service as men pleasers; but as the servants of Christ doing the will of God from the heart

Verse 7)
With good will doing service as to the Lord and not to men.

He would explain verse 6 and 7 like this, ... *"Ya'll shouldn't worry about what other people think about you obeying your leader, blessing and serving the man of God"* and furthermore that we should not bless him just to be seen like men pleasers but rather we should be willing to bless and serve the man of God because it is the will of God. In other words, keep it a secret. Can you believe that after hearing messages like this over and over again, the young women in the church, (married and single), including myself, would literally be in competition to see who could do the most for the man of God? Now, I know you are probably thinking, that is foul, and you are absolutely right, that was just down right out of line; but what's even worse is that he loved and worked it to his advantage. Yes, he was pimping from the pulpit.

He told us that the natural minded man would not understand how or why we would obey and serve the man of God in this manner, but he declared that God would bless us and keep us if we obeyed him and took care of him. Furthermore by obeying him we would always escape the wrath of God, because after all if you honor the prophet, you shall receive a prophet's reward.

Well, of course I didn't want any of the unfortunate things that he told us about the other people to happen to me, so leaving his church was ruled out as an option. I made up in my mind that I could accept instructions from the man of God and I could certainly be obedient, especially if it would please God, so I submitted myself under his authority trusting his every word. My desire was and still is to please God with all of me; however I submit that I was definitely mishandled as a babe in Christ. I believed in the man of God and trusted him with my life, but if I only knew what I know now... when he made the offer for us to leave and go find another Leader, I would have grabbed my coat, put on my running shoes and never looked back. Unfortunately I didn't know, so I fell for the Apostles presentation of the Gospel.

Even after hearing his mind-boggling sermons time and time again, I still didn't fully understand why he implied I was disobedient, about the trip I took to see my family. I believe it was because even though I had learned to obey his direct instructions he wanted me to obey even his suggestions.

I guess I couldn't imagine God being offended because I wanted to visit my family even though they didn't speak in tongues and prophecy. So the Apostles suggestion went in one ear and out the other. Wouldn't the Lord want me to go and be a witness?

Quite frankly I'm glad I didn't understand that I should obey his suggestions as if it were a direct instruction because I wanted to see my mom and so I went home. If I had only known what I know now, I would have run as fast as I could to get away from him. Before I knew it, ten years had passed as I sat under the auspices of this wayward man, who called himself an Apostle, and I lived in bondage all the while believing I was free in Christ. As a result I lost the tenacity to pursue my dreams, I was stripped of my keen ability to make decisions on my own and he, the Apostle, a 6-foot dirt creature became my god.

I guess you are wondering what happened to the young man that I met on the bus. Well, I will tell you ... I thought about him often, but I never called him, not after that spiritual beating that I took after my trip. However, approximately 20 days later he called me and my heart skipped a beat when I heard his voice on my answering service. I was afraid to call him back, but I did anyway, I guess I wasn't totally whipped into submission yet. He and I started dating, and we had a lot of fun together, as I said he kept me laughing and dreaming. Eventually things were getting a little bit more serious between us and for obvious reasons I wanted the Apostle to approve of him. So I told the Apostle about my friend and how I felt about him, then out of the blue, the Apostle said, "*bring him down to the church and let me see if he can preach".* Well, I was happy to hear that, and so was my friend when I told him that the Apostle had extended an invitation for him to come and speak. You see my friend was young in the ministry; he was a Preachers Kid, very well versed in scripture with a genuine desire to preach God's Word, so he gladly accepted the invitation. Boy! Were we in for a surprise? After my friend shared a rich message from the word of God about the woman with the issue of blood, and just when it seemed like everything had went well, the Apostle stood up in the pulpit and rebutted everything that he said and then concluded by saying,

"Just because he look good, and smell good, and he even spoke a good word, don't mean he's your husband"

He was apparently talking to me, and then the Apostle turned to my friend while he was sitting in the pulpit and said

"Boy, if you would just sit under my wings for little while, I'll help you, cause you got the Word but you need the POWER!!!"

Needless to say, I was embarrassed and humiliated. I thought to myself, why does he always have to say things that are so demeaning? But once again I sucked it up and dealt with it, after all what could I do about it. He was the Apostle, the Master-Builder, anointed and appointed and he was always right, right? Anyway, that event didn't stop my friend and me from seeing each other and after we talked about the event a few weeks later, we laughed about it and just let it go. In fact we are still friends today and we still laugh about it.

Well, the day soon came when the Apostle found out that I was still seeing him, and then the Apostle's true motives were revealed as he told me that my friend was trying to pull me out of the church, which simply was not true. Maybe he was trying to pull me out of THAT particular church, but certainly not out of the body of Christ. Anyhow the Apostle went on to say that I should stop seeing him, before I ended up burning. And it may sound funny, but I still didn't know what that meant and I was still afraid to ask.

As I stated before, I trusted the Apostle with my life. So I began to think that maybe he could see something spiritually unhealthy in my relationship with my friend that I couldn't see and maybe he's just looking out for my best interest. I didn't realize that I was slowly and meticulously being stripped and brought under total subjection to the Gospel according to the Apostle. I only wanted to be obedient to leadership and I certainly didn't want to be next Sunday's morning message. So to resolve any confusion I gradually stopped communicating with my friend.

After a short time apart, my friend called me on the phone and said something about the Apostle that I thought was so cruel. He said, *"Can't you see that the Apostle just wants you for himself?"* Well needless to say, I was offended and immediately on defense. I thought to myself, the nerve of him to talk that way about my leader, the man who teaches me the Word of God! And I was not going to just sit there and listen to him talk about the Apostle like that, so I defended my leaders character by saying, *"No, he is not that kind of man, he is a man of God!"* My friend said, *"Be that as it may, he is still a man with an agenda."* I was so perturbed after hearing all of this that I just ceased all communication with my friend from that day forward and I didn't speak with my friend again until Ten years later.

Chapter 5
Spiritual RAPE (Manipulation)

Have you ever heard the story about the man who was **trapped** on the rooftop of his house in the midst of a hurricane that had come and flooded the whole city? Well he was praying and believing that God would come and rescue him from this storm. Then all of a sudden, while he was waiting patiently for God to come, one of his neighbors came by in a boat to help him get to safety. The man adamantly refused the boat ride and with admirable confidence said, "God will come for me." Meanwhile, the man in the boat pleaded with the man on the rooftop, warning him of the danger that was coming his way but he still wouldn't get in the boat, so the man in the boat saved himself. Wouldn't you? Well a few hours passed while the flood-waters were still rising and then a rescue helicopter came for the man in a final attempt to save him. Again he unyieldingly refused the helicopter ride firmly declaring that God would come for him. Well as a result, the man on the rooftop drowned because he was so spiritually absorbed and misguided that he could not see God using carnal things like a boat or a helicopter to save him. In other words, he was so spiritual that he was no earthly good and the results were tragic. This story sheds light on how blind and ignorant I was when I failed to see that my one friend and many family members were trying to save me from spiritual abuse. My friend very boldly and directly warned me about the Apostle's fleshly intent towards me but I did not heed the warning. Then a few of my immediate family members said it seemed like I was part of a cult and yet I still did not take heed. Mom came to her conclusion after she noticed that I was losing my boldness, my creativity and the tenacity to pursue my dreams; while my sister honed in on my sudden personality conversion, which diverted from an outgoing, fun loving, innovative person into what society describes as an introvert. Both of my brothers expressed their concern when they mentioned they had never heard of a church where the Pastor told the members not to visit with their families, yet and still I ignored the red flags. By this time, I was so full of the Apostles philosophy that I could not taste the grits for the cheese, nor see the forest for the trees.

Well, after looking back with 20/20 hind sight and after an extended season of purging and spiritual maturity, I thought to myself, why couldn't I see what my loved ones were warning me about? What was wrong with me? And why in the world did I think my loved ones were my enemies? Well I will tell you why. The Apostle taught us that anyone who was not saved was the enemy including our family members. In fact, no one was saved, according to the Apostle, unless they agreed with his teachings. So by the time my family and friends tried to warn me, it was too late, I had already been hood winked. I couldn't fathom in my mind that the Apostle was wrong about anything because he was very influential and he always had a scripture from the bible to endorse his interpretation and doctrinal teaching of certain alleged Christian behavioral patterns. For example when I asked the Apostle why he thought it was not a good idea for me to visit my family, he responded with this scripture…

<u>2 Corinthians 6:17</u>
*Wherefore **come out from among them**, and be ye separate, saith the Lord, and touch not the unclean thing; and I will receive you.*

He explained that if I wanted the Lord to receive me I would have to be willing to forsake even my family because my family was not saved and they were a part of the world that I was supposed to separate myself from. The Apostle often stated in his sermons and in his conversation that he did not believe in **kin folk salvation**, meaning that once a person has given their life to Christ they were to have no regard for the thoughts of kinfolks or relatives that were not living holy. In other words, he was using the word of God meticulously separating us from our families. We were told that we had been adopted by God into a new family and furthermore that our natural family members could not comprehend what we had received from the Lord because we were chosen. Do you see the oxy moron here? He was right about the spiritual adoption into a new family according to the word of God,

Ephesians 2
[19]Now therefore ye are no more strangers and foreigners, but fellow citizens with the saints, and of the household of God;

However, he was wrong in his presentation of the scripture.

Many times the Apostles words just did not feel right in my spirit, and when I would get the nerve to ask a question about something he said, he would often respond by saying, "Now the student trying to teach the teacher". I would feel really stupid after he said that so eventually I stopped verbally questioning him about anything. After a while, I even stopped questioning his teachings in my mind because he was always somehow justified. Often times he would go overboard with being justified, in that even if his present conversation was contrary to something he had previously declared to be the truth according to the word of God, he was still justified because he would declare he had received a new revelation from God. There were numerous times when his life-style contradicted his teachings yet still I never opened my mouth to question the Apostles integrity because I was intimidated. *Intimidation* is driven by fear and is an enemy to prosperity causing the best of us to forfeit our dreams if we allow it to rule our lives. The Apostle taught us never to question him because he was the man of God, just obey him and God would bless us because obedience is better than sacrifice.

His philosophy eventually isolated us from friends, family, and even major events that were going on in the world. I spent ten years in spiritual confinement participating only in activities that directly involved our little church family. This may sound unbelievable but the only reason I knew about events like the Rodney King Riot or the OJ Simpson case is because I lived in Los Angeles and worked downtown near the courtroom where the Simpson trial actually took place.

You see, exposure endorses growth; while isolation hinders development, therefore control begins with separation or isolation. This tactic is used in prison and it is referred to as solitary confinement. It is designed to break the will of the inmates who have there own mind, to bring them under subjection to the rules and regulations of the institution. My question is; should the church operate with rules and regulations like a prison with the objective being to break the spirit of a person and bring the people of God subject to the leader or the rules of that church? Of course not,

John 8:36
³⁶*If the Son therefore shall make you free, ye shall be free indeed.*

1 Peter 5:2
²*Feed the flock of God which is among you, taking the oversight thereof, not by constraint, but willingly; not for filthy lucre, but of a ready mind;*

I submit that the solitary confinement method was indeed the same method used as the foundation of the doctrine taught by the Apostle, and as a result, those of us who trusted him with our lives became victims of spiritual hegemony.

MOTIVES and OPPORTUNITIES
Have you ever heard the question *"What is your M.O.?"* and wondered what it meant? Well, the unambiguous expression "M.O." as used in the question above simply means ----- *The procedures or routines for doing something, a method* - Motif and Operands or *Motive and Operation.*

Therefore, I submit that when the motive is **the desire for control**, and opportunity offers **someone who is vulnerable**, the M.O. is **"Power".**

The desire for power or control over someone else's life is to the church what a virus is to a computer system or what "aids" is to the human body. It breaks down the immune system and promotes a slow agonizing death.

By now you are probably saying to yourself, "this sister is bold", and I say to you, "Amen". You see, I've gathered the strength to write with boldness and declare the truth in this book because I love God's people, especially the babes in Christ. And it is my earnest desire to shed some light on the distinct differences between a submitted relationship with man versus and submitted relationship with God. I firmly believe that experience is the best teacher, so please learn from my experiences as you read this book and be free in the name of Jesus. Experience is the foundation on which I have written and shared in this manuscript thus far; with my hope in God that someone will be blessed and made free by reading my story. I am justified by faith to tell the truth without shame and I willingly do so, in Jesus name.

Romans 5
¹Therefore being justified by faith, we have peace with God through our Lord Jesus Christ:

²By whom also we have access by faith into this grace wherein we stand, and rejoice in hope of the glory of God.

³And not only so, but we glory in tribulations also: knowing that tribulation worketh patience;

⁴And patience, **experience; and experience, hope:**

*⁵***And hope maketh not ashamed***; because the love of God is shed abroad in our hearts by the Holy Ghost which is given unto us.*

Allow me to share an incident that happened to me in the church as a result of one mans need for power or control, and how it was only the grace of God that sustained me from dieing a slow agonizing spiritual and physical death.

SEX IN THE CHURCH and THE APOSTLE

At the tender age of twenty–two, a newborn babe in Christ, I was on fire for God because of all that He had done for me. I had zeal for God but not according to knowledge. I was married for little over a year to the young man that the Apostle suggested for me. And during this time, my husband and I were having some serious marital problems as a direct result of immaturity on both our parts. I was at my wits end and needed someone with life experience to talk to me. Now according to the word of God the older women are to teach the young women how to love their husbands.

Titus 2:4
4That they may teach the young women to be sober, to love their husbands, to love their children

Therefore, talking with one of the mothers in the church was definitely on my to-do list in an effort to get some help. However, in this church, under the leadership of the Apostle, things were a little bit different. Although he often quoted the appropriate scriptures from the bible, they took on a different meaning when the time came to act on what the scriptures say. Allow me to explain. You see we had two church mothers at the time, one who had three grown children but no husband and the other with four grown children and an unsaved husband. Here is the catch twenty-two; the Apostle would have someone read this scripture in Titus 2:4

and boldly state that the mothers should teach the young women how to love their husbands. Then all in the same breath he would declare and disqualify the two mothers, stating that neither one of them were qualified to teach the young women in our church how to love their husbands. He would take the liberty to point out that the one who had no husband certainly wasn't in a favorable position to teach young women how to love their husbands, and the other couldn't teach the young women in the church how to love a saved man because of the fact that her husband was not in the church. The only other aged woman in the church that the younger married women could possibly turn to for guidance was the Apostles wife, and he would disqualify her in his dissertations as he constantly exploited her weaknesses. I believe this was all part of his scheme to eliminate the young sisters' choices for counsel concerning our marriages. Accordingly, when ever there was trouble in any of our homes, no matter what the situation, married or single, male or female, young and old, we would turn to the Apostle for advice. As quiet as it has been kept, the 6-foot dirt creature that we all called Apostle had subconsciously taken the place of God.

Because of this teaching, when I was having problems in my marriage I went straight to the Apostle for counsel. Now, typically when we think of going to our Pastors or Leaders for counsel, it is the ideal thing to do, especially when it pertains to counsel for relationship issues.

Consequently, on this one very significant issue, when I called upon the Apostle for advice, he instructed me to come by the apartment where he and his wife lived. He said we could talk about my problems there. Now, just so you can see how naïve I was, it didn't phase me one way or the other that he wanted to counsel me at his residence during the day when his wife was at work. I really didn't think twice about it. However it is unusual, uncommon and certainly not wise for a Pastor to counsel a young woman in the comfort of his home during the day, when his wife is at work.

The Apostle was always available during the day because he didn't work. He says he was called to full time ministry because of the growth of our congregation; shucks I understand because we had grown to numbers unimaginable, unthinkable, and he just had to be available for the people full time. Boy! Let me tell you, we had approximately **twenty people *including* the children in our congregation, that's right, TWENTY whole people.** Ok... I'm being sarcastic, but it's true and I've got to tell you that the ministry never grew beyond twenty members in the ten years that I was there; and to my knowledge, that status still remains. Anyway, let me get back to what I was about to share. I imagine it was around 11:00 am in the morning when I went to see the Apostle for guidance on how to make my marriage better; nevertheless, my visit turned out to be more than a counseling session.

When I arrived at the one bedroom apartment in Inglewood, California, where he and his wife resided, he offered me a seat on the sofa in the living room, and then he said, "I'm listening" as he continued to iron the piece of clothing that he had yet to put on.

I began to tell the Apostle all about my troubles. I talked mostly about how weak and sorry I thought my husband was. I complained that he was not a man, and that he was immature and furthermore I was planning to leave him because I just couldn't take it anymore. I told the Apostle that I had over heard my husband and his mother talking and I heard my mother-in-law say that she wished her son would have married one of the other sisters in our church because she liked her better and my husband agreed. I went on and on, and as I continued my pity party, crying, sobbing, and blaming my husband for everything that was going wrong in our marriage I felt better, not because I was right, but because someone was finally listening to me.

Honestly I expected the Apostle to show me some scriptures in the bible that would point out my own personal mistakes so I could re-evaluate the situation and not place all the blame on my husband or at least give me some sound advice on what I could do to make things more peaceful at home. On the contrary, he began to agree with me about my husband, telling me that I married a boy and not a man.

And at some point in the conversation he told me that I needed to learn how to make myself happy. He used a sexual innuendo to explain what he meant as if sex is the foundation of marriage. He asked me if I knew how a prostitute was able to work the streets, lay with many different men and retain her strength.

Well, needless to say, I couldn't answer the question, given the fact that I'd never entertained that life style. So he explained by saying, "she doesn't release herself because she knows she is working", He further explained that if the prostitute wanted to release herself she would come back and make love to her pimp. Ok, you are probably thinking, "where is this conversation going?" Well, if it's any comfort to you, I was wondering too.

As I told you before, it was always a challenge for me to follow the Apostles conversation because he jumped around a lot, changing from one subject to another. He would conveniently throw in a scripture whenever it was necessary to back up what he was saying, knowing that I would never dispute the word of God. He constantly used parables to paint a picture that would explain his theory, always cross referencing his philosophy with a scripture from the Bible. So, needless to say, by the time I was preparing to leave his place, and after talking with him, I really didn't know what we had specifically talked about.

I remember standing by the door with my purse and bible in hand as I waited for him to walk me out to my car. He stood up and walked over to the door where I stood then he embraced me. Now the embrace was not unusual, until it became inappropriate when he began to touch me intimately, placing his hand in the small of my back and then whispering these words in my ear, "Don't be scared."

It was apparent that I was very uncomfortable and nervous, so lets be real, this kind of interaction with a Pastor is definitely unusual and wrong. So, as I stood there trembling with my heart racing, he gently backed away from me, never taking his eyes off me. As he sat down in the chair he softly said, "Take them off."

I just knew he couldn't be talking about my clothes right? Wrong. That's exactly what he was talking about. I was scared to death because I couldn't fathom in my mind what made him think I wanted to take my clothes off. Questions immediately began running through my mind and I blamed myself for his actions, Oh my God! What had I done to entice the Apostle? Was my dress to short? Did I smile too much? What? What did do? As I stood there stiff as a board, he repeated himself saying, "Go ahead take them off" as if it were alright or as if he thought I was alright with his request. He wasn't forceful in his approach in fact his actions were very gentle yet I was afraid to say no. Now I know you are probably thinking why would I be afraid to say **no**? Well I believe it was because I had never told him **no** about anything before, in fact **no** was not part of my vocabulary when it came to the Apostle. So when I thought **no**, that word just wouldn't come out of my mouth. I was frozen stiff and couldn't move or speak; I just stood there like a scared little girl, trying to comprehend what was going down. The Apostle stood up and slowly walked back over toward me, and gently took my purse and my bible out of my hands placing them on the floor near my feet. He began to unbutton my blouse and then he proceeded to caress the silhouette of my body pulling me close to him.

I was like a puppet on strings as I heeded to his every move. At that moment, I began experiencing some serious mixed emotions as he unveiled himself in my presence preparing to lay with me. I was definitely intimidated and afraid to tell the Apostle to stop; it was as if I was under some kind of spiritual restraint. I wanted to tell him that I had no desire for him this way, because he was like my dad, in fact I even called him dad at times. Nevertheless, I have to be honest with myself; there was a part of me that craved for the intimate attention that he was apparently willing to give. You see I wanted and needed the intimate attention but I did not want sex with him. If you can fathom this analogy in your mind, imagine this. On one hand I felt like a homeless person who was grateful because this man had given me a warm blanket of intimacy after all those cold nights with my husband, while at the same time I felt like a prostitute being held down in a dark alley by two men and then being helplessly injected with a heroine needle. I wanted to say no and couldn't, I wanted to run and wouldn't, I wanted to scream and be heard, but yet I didn't even mumble one word.

WHY and HOW?

Why, Why, Why? How, How, How? Why and how did this end up happening time and time again? Yes... it happened more than once.

Well after the first time he touched me, I remember walking into the church on the following Sunday morning feeling as if I was sitting in a first class seat to hell. I felt like a heathen, my heart was heavy, and the emotional weight of the burden that I carried was sapping the very life out of me. As I sat in the Sunday morning service going through the motions, I watched the Apostle stand boldly in the pulpit preaching really hard until sweat was pouring from his body. He was going on and on as if everything was all right and as if all was well with his soul. However, I was having a hard time just sitting there, my hearing was dull, and I felt separated from my God. I had never experienced any problems or struggles entering into the presence of the Lord because I am a worshipper. However, this day, I was suffering as a result of the guilt and the shame that flooded my mind. With a sad countenance on my face and my head held down in disgrace, I began praying and repenting to the Lord saying, "Please forgive me and help me". Now anyone who knew me would know that there had to be something terribly wrong because I'm always in high spirits with a smile on my face no matter what the situation.

I tried desperately to gather my thoughts so I could get involved in the service. I wanted to praise

God and feel His presence, but no matter how hard I tried, I could not escape my conscience. I felt dirty and violated and I was convicted in my spirit. I needed to hear a word from the Lord because my heart was burdened for a break through. I didn't know what to do, so I cried out to the Lord and I know He heard me because suddenly I felt an urgency in my spirit to get up and go lay my burden down on the alter.

So I moved quickly, throwing myself on the alter I began to thank God for his mercy as I felt some relief. In the background, I could hear the Apostle getting louder and louder in the microphone as if he were trying to drown out my praise because I came boldly before the thrown of grace and I was letting my request be known, as I was telling the Lord how sorry I was for my indiscretions and I was thanking God for his mercy and for his forgiveness. I didn't care if the people in the church could hear what I was saying, I was seeking God for deliverance.

Then abruptly, in the midst of my praise, the Apostle walked over to the alter where I lay, grabbed me by one of my arms and pulled me up off the alter. I was weak and my knees were like rubber as I tried to gather myself. I didn't understand why he would interrupt my time of worship on the alter because I was on the brink of the breakthrough that I needed. I couldn't figure out what he was doing. Then while he held my arm firmly in his hand, he shook my body as if I were a dusty rag doll and said with a very authoritative voice, as he looked me in my red, swollen, teary eyes, "Woman, get up off this alter and shake yourself". At that moment, I swear I felt transference of spirit, because suddenly I felt no conviction, I wiped my eyes and walked back to my seat. After that day, whenever he saw an opportunity to lay with me, he took advantage of it. This went on for approximately three to four months from Los Angeles to Philadelphia. He took me on the evangelistic field with him to preach the Gospel of Jesus Christ and all the while he continued to spiritually and physically assault me. Now some looking from the outside would declare that we were committing adultery, but if you had the spiritual capacity to look from the inside, you would understand that it was indeed spiritual rape and manipulation. I had no conscience and I was becoming content with our little secret because I was overtaken by his spirit and ruled by his authority, not to mention that I felt like there was nothing I could do about it. However, my day of deliverance was soon to come when one of my prayer partners confronted me about the whole situation. She boldly challenged my calling to the ministry asking me what was hindering me from flowing in the anointing like I use to. She told me that she had always admired the anointing on my life, saying that my gifts in ministry reminded her of her younger days. She went on to say that, she had a dream about me and in the dream, she saw the Apostle on top of me. That's right, I said on top of me... OK..... Stop and breathe. Oh my God! I almost fainted because she made that statement boldly looking directly in my eyes. How could I lie to her, when I knew it wasn't her speaking to me, there is no way she could have known unless the living God revealed this to her. It was undoubtedly God speaking through her, reaching out for my soul, giving me another chance to come clean. The word of God says ...

Revelation 3:18-20

¹⁹As many as I love, I rebuke and chasten: be zealous therefore, and repent.

²⁰Behold, I stand at the door, and knock: if any man hear my voice, and open the door, I will come in to him, and will sup with him, and he with me.

This was my opportunity to repent be made free. Wow! My God is awesome and His mercy endureth forever. He has so much compassion and love for us that even in the midst of sinful living, He chastens, rebukes, and encourages our hearts to repent and be made whole. His love and the blood of Jesus constantly cleanse us from all unrighteousness. It just amazes me every time I think about how He directs our path and how God himself could not and would not allow me to continue walking in the error of my way. I was blinded by manipulation, overtaken by temptation, being ruled by the arm of the flesh, and dieing a slow spiritual and physical death. But God made a way of escape for me. Hallelujah!

1 Corinthians 10:13

¹³There hath no temptation taken you but such as is common to man: but God is faithful, who will not suffer you to be tempted above that ye are able; but will with the temptation also make a way to escape, that ye may be able to bear it.

Anyhow, when my prayer partner boldly challenged me to come clean and expose my wrongdoing, she charged me to take responsibility for my own actions. There was a serious war going on between my flesh and the spirit, because I had entered into contentment with this sin. However, no matter how agonizing and embarrassing it seemed to be for me to expose this sin that had overwhelmed my life, I couldn't deny the opportunity to be made free.

When I tried to open my mouth and deny that her allegations were factual, I stumbled over my words and broke down as I began to weep and wail from the depths of my soul because of the overwhelming sorrow that I felt as I realized how much God must love me. As I was slumped over weeping, my cry had a depth to it that I had never experienced before. It felt as if the virtue was being constricted out of my very soul as I cried out saying, "he won't stop, I can't tell him no".

My prayer partner wrapped her arms around me as she held me up and began praying for God to strengthen me. I kept crying out saying, "he won't stop, I can't say no to him" My prayer partner then said with authority, "What do you mean, you can't say no to him!" I kept crying out the words "I can't, I just can't" She shook me and said, "**Yes you can!**" Then she began to speak to the spirit of fear that had gripped my soul and made residence in my life, boldly declaring that "God has not given us the spirit of fear, but of love, power and a sound mind, and I command you spirit of fear and all of your supporting imps to come out in Jesus name and I command the spirit of love, power and a sound mind to take authority over this woman of God now!" Whew! Immediately I dropped to my knees as I felt a release in my spirit. When she finished praying for me, something changed in my spirit. As I sat there with my prayer partner drying my weeping eyes, she said to me, "The next time that man wants to put his filthy hands on you inappropriately, just say **no**; and the more you say no, the easier it will be". It was then that I realized that I never wanted him to touch me in the first place. What I really wanted was to feel loved and appreciated, I wanted companionship; and in some twisted, deceived kind of way, when I was sexually involved with the Apostle, the void in my life seemed to be temporarily filled. It was like a drug addiction, something that is terribly destructive yet deceivingly desirable.

Well the day soon came when the Apostle reached out to me for another booty call. When I answered the phone, he said four little words that use to have power over my body and my mind. Those words were "Bring it to me". How degrading is that? Anyhow, he spoke those words with much confidence as if my vagina was a piece of merchandise that I carried around all day waiting to deliver to him upon his command. Well, this was the day that the Apostle lost his power over me, because of my willingness to be made free. Yes, I said my willingness to be free; you see if you don't want to be free, you will remain in bondage, it's that simple. Therefore, when he spoke those words to me over the phone, I did not heed to his call as in times past; In fact, before I could bat an eye, the little two-letter word that use to be so unattainable, unreachable and unachievable came effortlessly out of my mouth, as I boldly uttered the powerful word, NO. Wow.... I actually said no to the Apostle. Now I know that might sound absolutely insane to you, but it was a great achievement and victory for me. I could tell that he was shocked and at a loss for words, because there was a moment of silence on the other end of the phone just before he asked me to repeat what I had just said. Therefore, I obliged him and said it again, no. He couldn't believe that I said no to him, in fact, I couldn't believe that I said no to him either, but I did, and it felt really good.

I could tell that it took a few minutes for him to process the reality of losing control and I assume he had to deal with the whole idea of me finally saying no to him. He had to be as shocked as I was, if not more based on his response. I imagine it was almost like being cursed out, without an explanation. However when he realized that I was not giving heed to his request and I had actually said no, and meant it, he appallingly said, "Who are you giving it to now?" Oh my God, can you believe that? Well, my weave was blown back after he made that statement and I was absolutely sickened, and disgusted by his words. Some part of me wanted curse him out, and then I wanted to question him about how he could or why he would ask me such a degrading question, but I just left it alone because that was in his heart and in his mind. When I realized that, my heart was comforted by this scripture...

Proverbs 23:7
⁷For as he thinketh in his heart, so is he: Eat and drink, saith he to thee; but his heart is not with thee.

After I had finally found the strength to say no to him, I needed to know what the next step was to move in the direction of total freedom and deliverance from this spiritual hegemony. I wanted to know what it felt like to walk in an environment that was spiritually conducive for my growth in the Lord. An environment that was uncontrolled by the bondage that resulted from the kind of philosophy taught by the Apostle that I sat under for ten years. I was afraid and without counsel concerning this matter. Fear tried desperately to grip my heart again as I thought of just leaving the church all together. I was worried that if I just stopped coming to church, everyone, including my husband would start asking questions that I wasn't eager to answer. You see, after all of this, I still didn't want to expose the Apostle or myself, I just wanted to get out and be free. But, I soon found out that one sure way to be made free is to expose the devil because he can't work in the light. My hearts desire was to get my life back on track with God so that I could re-capture that special anointing that once saturated my life.

GUILTY CONSCIENCE

A guilty conscience is like a shadow or a dark spirit that hovers over our lives constantly reminding us of our wrong doings. The only way to defeat a guilty conscience is through the blood of Jesus Christ, which was shed for the remission of our sins. When we know we are wrong and the opportunity to confess our sins arises, if we refuse the love we will remain in bondage as a slave to sin. However, the bible says...

1 John 1:9
9If we confess our sins, he is faithful and just to forgive us our sins, and to cleanse us from all unrighteousness.

The guilt of sin promotes two very dangerous options, **fear** and **self justification**. You see, fear and self-justification are two of the many reasons that we end up hurting others in the process of trying to conceal our own wicked ways.

For example, when the Apostle realized that our little fiasco was really over, he was overcome with fear and desperation, which lead to self justification because he wouldn't confess the truth and he didn't want to change. To tell the truth was just too much like the right thing to do. And, because he was filled with self righteousness, when the opportunity for repentance was presented, he denied the love of God.

Instead of just telling the truth and going through the process of being cleansed and made whole, not only did he choose to lean on the arm of the flesh denying the truth, he is still holding on to that lie today. The Apostle declares that he never touched me at all, and has even invented a story that makes him appear squeaky clean. He has creatively and publicly made false allegations concerning my alleged actions. He claims that I made a special trip to his church in California and openly repented to him in front of the congregation. He maintains that I openly repented for lying on him. I have to say that I was not surprised to hear about this story from a very reliable source; however I am absolutely amazed at how far he has gone to cover up this sin. Wow!

Anyhow, as the light began to shine more and more on this messy situation, he began to use his perpetrated position of authority to tear down my credibility just in case I was planning to expose the truth about what really happened between us. Who would have ever thought that I would have the courage to write it in a book?

The Apostle often used the pulpit to send subliminal messages to me and others through his sermons. I believe his hope in doing this was to pump fear into our hearts and put a lock on our jaw. I remember when he once preached a sermon from the book of Samuel about David and Bathsheba. I believe his full intent was to send a direct message to me, warning me to keep my mouth shut. Allow me to break it down for you scripture by scripture.

2 Samuel 11:2-5 & 15
The scripture says:

²And it came to pass in an evening tide, that David arose from off his bed, and walked upon the roof of the king's house: and from the roof he saw a woman washing herself; and the woman was very beautiful to look upon.

Apostle's interpretation: Bathsheba knew that king David would be walking upon the roof top, and she knew she was beautiful so she purposely planned to wash herself where he could see her nakedness, with intentions to entice the King to call for her to lay with him. In other words, she trapped the King.

The scripture says:

³And David sent and enquired after the woman. And one said, Is not this Bathsheba, the daughter of Eliam, the wife of Uriah the Hittite?

Apostle's interpretation: Bathsheba was happy when she found out that the king was enquiring about her. She couldn't wait to get into the Kings quarters to lay with him even though she was married. She wanted to be with the king, because her husband was a "poot butt".

- ***Poot Butt*** is another creative word phrase often used by the Apostle to describe a man who is inadequate when it pertains to taking care of a woman.

The scripture says:

⁴And David sent messengers, and took her; and she came in unto him, and he lay with her; for she was purified from her uncleanness: and she returned unto her house.

Apostle's interpretation: David said a few words and found out that the woman was glad to lay with him, in fact she was waiting for his call and then she washed herself and went home like nothing happened, because she had got what she wanted, "the King".

*NOTE

The Scriptures depict:

After David had sent for Uriah's wife Bathsheba, and after he had lain with her, David received a letter from Bathsheba saying that she had conceived a child. Well how could a married woman conceive a child when her husband is off to battle in a war, unless she was unfaithful? King David attempted to cover up his sin, because he realized there were witnesses that knew he had lain with her and that her husband wasn't around. There would be only one logical explanation for this conception and David knew it would only be a matter of time before nature would reveal that the woman was with child. So King David wanted it to appear as though it was Uriah the husband who fathered the child. So King David sent for Uriah and ordered him to go and lay with his wife. However Uriah was a faithful warrior and he loved David so much that he couldn't bring himself to think about laying with his wife while his brethren were in war. So instead of going in to lay with his wife, he lay at King David's door and slept there all night. So when King David found out that

Uriah had not lain with his wife, he was angered because he knew his sin would soon be exposed because his cover up plan didn't work. So, sadly as a result of the King's guilt and anger ...

... The scripture says:

[15]And he wrote in the letter, saying, Set ye Uriah in the forefront of the hottest battle, and retire ye from him, that he may be smitten, and die.

Apostle's interpretation: the woman wanted King David, to have her husband killed because after she had been pleasingly touched by the King she didn't want to go home to her sorry, "poot butt" husband.

After all of this continued nonsense, it was clear to me that the Apostle was obviously not willing to change and get it right. He continued to twist the word of God in his attempt to make me feel guilty as he suggested in his dissertation that I was even as Bathsheba washing myself naked in his eyesight, with a burning desire for him to lay with me and get rid of my husband. Sound silly? I know, but it is true. You see, his interpretation was delivered in such a way that if I was not trusting God for complete deliverance from this madness, I would have been hood-winked all over again. Nevertheless, I thank God for Jesus and for delivering me out of the mouth of this lion even as he did for Daniel when he was in the lions den.

Things to Do, to avoid Spiritual Hegemony

- **Be careful concerning the seeds/ or words that you allow people to plant in your life**
- **Don't allow anyone to Isolate you, exposure enhances your mind.**

- **Study and understand God's Word for yourself so you can minimize the chances of being Manipulated or taken advantage of.**
- **What ever you give, whether it is your money, your time, your energy etc... Always give as unto the Lord and he will protect you.**
- **Be watchful with whom you lend your Confidence**
- **Always Pray, for the Word of God says Men should always pray and not faint.**

Making Conscience Decisions

Wow! After all, of these years I had finally come into the knowledge of the truth, the eyes of my understanding had been enlightened. I realized that the foundation of this *particular* Apostle's doctrine was cause for the conflict in my spirit and I simply refused to stay there any longer.

Inwardly I was so grateful that God had cleansed and renewed my spirit, but in actuality I was still attending this church, sitting there yet in another service. As I sat there, I remember feeling imprisoned by these church walls as if I couldn't just get up and get out. I felt spiritually forced to be there to listen to this Apostle as he continued to distort God's Word with his philosophy. I felt physically trapped even though I had been spiritually and emotionally enlightened. What was I supposed to do now? The answer was simple, I had to make a choice, and so I chose to leave. It was clearly understood that it was time for me to move up and out of this situation and God had finally given me enough strength to just walk away.

Nevertheless, even after all of the hurt, deception and my decision to leave, I still didn't have the heart to expose the Apostle. Now I know you may be thinking, Why not? Well, it was because I had been blessed with the gifts to forgive and to love without boundaries. I was **better** as a result of being freed from this bondage and not **bitter**. Another reason is because I saw him as a weak man made of flesh and blood who was in desperate need of God's mercy just like the rest of us. And besides all of that, who am I to judge another man's servant? My hearts desire was and has always been to see people happy and prosperous, not down trodden or scandalized. I only wanted to move on, so I told my husband that I wanted to leave this church, in fact I wanted to leave the state of California, but he was sold on the fictitious, fabricated, conjured thought that there was no one in the world who could preach better than the Apostle. Well, I became very indignant about leaving and searching for a place that would be conducive for sound spiritual growth and advancement. However, my husband didn't want to leave, in fact he stated many times that he wanted to be just like the Apostle. It was then that I knew he didn't have a clue about what was really going on. Over and over again, my husband and I engaged in the redundant, lifeless conversation about staying or leaving, but my mind was made up, I was leaving. My husband continued to try and reason with me about staying but his conversation was to no avail. As a result, I soon became very frustrated and angered because of what I knew. Perhaps I should have told him at that time, why I was so desperate to get away however, I chose not to disclose that information because I thought the pain that I had been dealing with on my own was enough. My husband was firm on staying there as a result of my failure to speak openly. Nevertheless I still refrained from telling him the truth about why I wanted to leave, and as a result I became even more frustrated. I told my husband that I was leaving and if he wasn't coming with me, he could consider himself left.

Needless to say, I was finished talking about it, I realized that it was time to do something about it. So I went out and rented a U-Haul truck and began to load up. When my husband saw this he realized that I was serious and decided to come with me to Las Vegas. Upon arriving in Las Vegas, I was somewhat comforted in that I already knew where I was going to live, temporarily that is. Please understand that Las Vegas is my home, the place where I was born and raised. My mother told me that if I ever needed a place to lay my head, as long as she was living, I could always come back home, so I did.

Consequently, I also knew what church we would be attending. You see, one of the associate ministers who attended the Apostles church in LA with us, had left approximately one year before us and started his own ministry in Las Vegas. I was excited about being a part of a new ministry, especially this one in particular because he was the same minister that first introduced me to Christ. When he left LA, I was hurt because I felt like he left me there with the big bad wolf, (the Apostle) to fin for myself. I desperately wanted to leave also, but apparently it wasn't my time. Nevertheless, when the opportunity for departure finally came, and the decision to move to Vegas was secured, I thought his church would be somewhat of a safe haven. I believed his church would be a place where I could actually receive spiritual healing. I thought for sure he would understand the nature of the pain that I had suffered under the Apostles ministry because he and his family were also victims of the same spiritual hegemony and manipulation. I was under the impression that he took his family and left California because he wanted a fresh start. Boy was I in for the shock of my life as I realized that the fruit didn't fall that far from the tree.

Allow me to explain. You see, I served under the auspices of this new ministry in Las Vegas for approximately one year. While working diligently in ministry, hoping, praying and believing God for better things; I found out that this young Pastor had also mastered the art of spiritual manipulation and was industriously working his craft. He was operating like what I would describe as "the Apostle Jr." with the nerve to try and take that tainted doctrine to the next level. Shucks, I remember when this young leader had no apparent fear or reverence for God as he would stand in the pulpit and boldly call the saints of God vulgar names like niggers and whores. Unlike the Apostle, instead of preaching in parables about the hell he was personally involved in, and then leaving it up to the congregation to figure it out; this young leader was so bold that he would stand flat footed in the pulpit and straight out tell you what he was doing. If you didn't like it, he would dance in your face and often use this phrase, "The doors of this church swings both ways", in fact that was the church motto. Now, stop and think for a minute, did he really believe that he could build a church on lies and deceit in Jesus' name? Hmm? I wonder. Well whether he did or not, God said no! Bless His holy name and thank Him for His mercy.

God says in His Word that His Grace is sufficient ...

2 Corinthians 12:9
And he said unto me, My **grace is sufficient**
for thee: for my strength **is** *made perfect in*
weakness. Most gladly therefore will I rather glory

in my infirmities, that the power of Christ may rest upon me.

... Thank God for His sufficient Grace in all things and thank God for his Grace and mercy concerning this young Pastor. He was apparently operating on a weak and manipulated mindset, which I believe was a manifestation of the residue from the teaching that he had sat under for almost 15 years. I am proud to report that because this young Pastor was and is indeed a man after God's own heart; he could not and was not permitted to continue this masquerade of ministry. God Himself eventually closed the doors to this church that was located in Las Vegas, changed this young leader's direction to give him a fresh start, and scattered the flock which included my baby sister. She testifies today, that when I left her in this church, she felt the same way I did when this same Pastor left me in California with the Apostle.

Nevertheless, God still sits on the throne and through much prayer He has directed my baby sister to a fruitful ministry where she has grown and matured spiritually; a place where she is experiencing frequent manifestations of the power and love of God. Hallelujah!

During the time that I was still attending the Las Vegas church, and experiencing this spiritual manipulation for the second time around, *(first in LA at the mercy of the Apostle and then in Las Vegas at the mercy of "the Apostle Jr."),* I had made contact with my special friend from ten years ago. This was the same friend who warned me about the intentions of the Apostle back in the year 1988. I hadn't seen my friend for approximately ten years, so we had a lot of catching up to do. And even though it felt good to finally be in touch with my friend again, I was very hesitant and reluctant to visit, that is when I considered the state of turmoil that my life was in at that time. Honestly, I was completely embarrassed to meet face to face with my friend after all of these years from (1988 – 1998), because I had accomplished nothing. On the contrary my friend had accomplished many notable things and had become a national artist. You see, we'd shared our dreams and visions and encouraged one another to let nothing stop us from embracing a prosperous future. We vowed that we would allow our creative gifts in ministry to catapult us to great heights according to the will of God.

Shamefully for me, over those past ten years, the only testimony that I had to share with my friend was how much abuse I had suffered in the church and that I was sorry for not giving heed to the warning given about the Apostles intentions toward me. But, my friend's creatively witty God given gifts had opened doors that allowed the achievement of national artist status.

Now, even though I was ashamed to visit with my friend because I had not achieved anything with my gifts, I decided to fly to the Washington DC area for a visit anyway. Oh what a blessing it was, because this turned out to be the trip that changed the course of my life. During that blessed visit with my friend, I was shown some tough love. My friend boldly and quite frankly told me that if I wanted to see better things happen in my life, I needed to get away from pigeons and run with the eagles. After hearing such a profound use of words, I had many questions concerning that statement. I wanted to know what the characteristics of a pigeon were, vs. the characteristics of an eagle; and how to apply the principle of this statement to my life. I received the answers that I needed to gather the understanding, and it was then that I decided that when I return to Vegas, I was not going to sit under a cursed ministry any longer and it was much easier for me to leave that time.

I remember it was a Sunday morning, after I returned from Washington DC, when I shared with my husband what was really going on. I told him that I was not going back to that church, but he didn't take me serious and just laughed in my face saying "yeah right, you'd better get up and get ready for church". Even so, I continued my dissertation, finally sharing the details about what happened between the Apostle and me in California prior to moving to Vegas. I went on to tell him that the same "stuff" that transpired in California was being replicated here in Vegas, only I was not the victim this time. Well, even though it took my husband a few minutes to process the information that I had given him, after he thought about some of the things that I stated, and realized certain undisputable truths, it was then that he expressed great anger as he tried to punch a hole in the wall. I imagine if the Apostle had been there at that very moment that punch would have landed on his jaw instead of the wall. I sat there wondering what my husband was thinking, then suddenly his demeanor changed and his anger was redirected towards me. He looked at me with a frown on his face breathing only through his nostrils and said very sternly with a demeaning tone, "You always wanted him". Whew! That hurt. I was dumb with silence after he made that statement, so I just sat there and said nothing. I was so spiritually numbed to the point that I had no more fight in me; I really didn't care what he or anyone else thought at that moment, I was tired. I knew within myself that I had kept all of this "stuff" bottled up inside of me, all of this time, in an effort to protect his feelings; all the while killing myself. I had been battling with self esteem, suicidal thoughts, self condemnation, and depression. I suffered through sleepless night continuously tormented because subconsciously I thought and believed in my heart that what happened between me and the Apostle was entirely my fault. And now that I had finally gathered the strength and the boldness to just tell my husband what was really going on, all he could say was "You always wanted him"? It was then I realized that this young man was merely someone that I'd married, he was not my husband.

"I believe a husband is sensitive to the practical and spiritual needs of his rib and has been given the uncanny ability to love without boundaries. A husband liberally and wisely exercises the authority given to him by God for covering and protecting his wife. Additionally a "husband" is perfectly designed to Love, Nurture, Encourage, and Comfort his wife; furthermore he is spiritually, emotionally, physically and economically equipped by God for the commitment and the responsibility of being a husband."

Although the man I married was a nice young man, with a heart of gold, he was not equipped for the call of duty as a "husband" at that time. This is why he was unable to sense the presence of another man taking advantage of his wife and ruling his house from the outside.

After a decade of marriage he was still **not** ready to be a husband, and I was finished playing house. I needed to find myself, I needed to know who I was and whose I was, I needed to find out why God made me, I needed to know my purpose. So shortly thereafter, I left that church and soon separated from this perpetrator who posed as my husband for ten years. I left abruptly because the lack of understanding on both our parts provoked a very hostile environment. As a result, things swiftly escalated from verbal abuse to physical abuse, and common sense would dictate that this was not a conducive atmosphere for the maturity of our daughter or my health. Thank God for common sense and for the strength to move on.

Subsequently I was saddened and I felt defeated and isolated, because after ten years of marriage, it appeared that all I had to show for it was a broken heart. Well at least that is all I thought I had to show for ten years of marriage; that is until I looked into the eyes of my beautiful daughter who became my inspiration to live after I realized that God had blessed me to be a mother; whew! What an awesome gift!

I made up in my mind that I was going to be the best mother that I could be and no one could take that away from me, flesh of my flesh and bones of my bones. I became determined with urgency to teach her that she could make it in this life no matter what, because the word of God says...

Isaiah 54:17
No weapon *that is* **formed** *against thee shall prosper; and every tongue that shall rise against thee in judgment thou shalt condemn. This is the heritage of the servants of the LORD, and their righteousness is of me, saith the LORD.*

I realized that the only way I could teach her this shrewd lesson of life was to live it before her, and so the awesome undertaking of motherhood became the primary focus of my mission and my ministry. Hallelujah!

After the separation, my daughter and I went through and faced some very hard times. We faced struggle after struggle, with no money, no child support, no job and living in the back room of my mother's house. I was fighting depression with every ounce of my dwindling strength.

I began hopping from church to church dragging my precious little girl everywhere I went; looking for some love, some freedom, some help. Where was God in all of this? I couldn't find Him anywhere; I felt like Job, after he lost everything and had to deal with all of those miserable comforters.

<u>Job 16:2</u>
I have heard many such things: **miserable comforters** *are ye all.*

There were people on every side, speaking with anger, whispering among themselves and some who were even bold enough to get in my face and openly voice there opinions about why I was going through all of this drama.

Nevertheless, I stumbled through my tears, blinded by mixed emotions until one day God lead me into one very special ministry. It was on a Sunday morning as the Pastor of this very intimate loving church was delivering his sermon, the same church that my baby sister now attends. I sat down in the back of the church and listened attentively as the Pastor continued to deliver his message. I remember feeling the overwhelming presence of God in this church as the Pastor was speaking. Then abruptly, yet peacefully and in accordance with the Spirit of the living God, the Pastor stopped in the middle of his message, looked directly at me and said, "Daughter, can I pray for you?" Immediately fear gripped my heart and my entire body was tense as I began to look around suggesting with my body language, *"Are you talking to me?"* The Pastor replied very gently to my gestures, saying "Yes daughter, you; can I pray for you?" Even though I could clearly hear the earnest desire and compassion in his voice crying out for my soul, fear had gripped my heart because after all that I had been through, I was persuaded that I could trust no one, especially Pastors. While I sat there bound and oppressed by fear, unable to speak or move, the Pastor slowly stepped out of the pulpit and moved meticulously toward me. As he walked cautiously in my direction with his arms outstretched, anger began to speak to my heart and tears began to cloud my vision. I began uncontrollably weeping as I cried out these words, "Leave me alone!" The Pastor tenderly said, "I'm not going to hurt you". He then called for his wife, instructing her to embrace me. I allowed her to do so only because she did not violate my personal space with overzealous spirituality. On the contrary, the woman of God used wisdom and was very polite in her approach as she sat down next to me and asked for my permission to embrace me. When she wrapped her loving arms around me, I felt safe, I felt loved, I felt freedom and I felt protected. The power of this loving hug was utterly amazing because as I closed my eyes, it felt like God Himself was embracing me. This extraordinary hug was filled with the kind of compassion that would enable me to comfortably take off the "happy mask" ultimately unveiling my broken heart and contrite spirit. I began to weep and whale uncontrollably for an extended period of time saying, "I don't know what to do" and while I was weeping, I could hear the Pastors voice in the background saying "I command you to release her in Jesus' name". He began to call out to the spirits depression and fear saying, "Devil, you are the father of liars and you have no authority over her life, and I command you to loose your hold in Jesus' name." I didn't know what was happening to me at that time, but it sure felt good, hallelujah! After I'd calmed down a little bit, the Pastor asked me if I could stand up; at first I didn't think so because I felt so weak, but then the Pastors wife assisted me in erecting to my feet. As I stood there looking directly into the eyes of this fearless Pastor, he uttered these very profound words "Daughter, you've got to forgive yourself". Suddenly the congregation was as quiet as a mouse and anyone could tell that they were intensely listening and waiting with anticipation to hear what it was that I needed to forgive myself for. But then the Pastor discerned the spirit of the church and abruptly turned toward the musicians telling them to play and then instructed the people to pray as he hastily put down the microphone expressing urgency to speak to me. Then suddenly this man of God gently placed his big hands on both my cheeks, leaned over and whispered in my ear so that only I could hear him say, "You've been asking God a few questions about your life and your destiny, and God says, he needs you to forgive yourself". Then just when I was questioning in my mind, exactly what it was that I needed to forgive myself for; The Pastor went on to say, "Quit blaming yourself, you were spiritually and physically raped and then made to believe it was your fault, but it was not your fault, you did not ask for this assault and you need to forgive yourself, so God can raise you up." Wow! How could he have known what I had been through and that this was my struggle? This Pastor didn't know me ... Oh my God! It was at that moment I realized God was answering my prayers through this man, instructing me of what I needed to do for complete deliverance. Whew! Upon realizing this phenomenon, I fell down and lay prostrate on the alter, in the presence of the Lord and began to worship. Glory to God! I knew it was not this man speaking to me, but it was God, and in due season I had received my deliverance as I was freely given the bread of life. I will always Praise God for using this man of God and for exemplifying the ministry of His Glory!

Chapter 6
Walking Into My Destined Place
(A Pathway through Tribulation to Triumph)
(The Valley of the Shadows of Death, The Pathways of Righteousness)

My Pathway

From outstanding achievements to prison, from divine intercession to spiritual manipulation, from a free spirit to holy bondage, from sacred chastity to religious rape, from pathetic ignorance to devout understanding and finally from tribulation to triumph. Now that's quite a pathway, one that would have been impossible to end in triumph without the Lord on my side. Thank God for Jesus.

As you have read thus far, I have been blessed to miraculously overcome **all** of the obstacles that were presented to me on this purposed pathway. However, in times past I would not have described my pathway with the word purposed, because it felt like the pathway to hell. Nonetheless, I now understand that my pathway was and is purposed because my life displays the manifestation and unveils the revelation of Romans 8:28. Today, I testify that all things work together for my good because I am called according to His purpose.

A New Season A New Day
Me, Myself and I

When I realized my call to ministry, I didn't know exactly what I was being called to do nor did I know why God would want to use someone like me, but I knew for sure I was chosen.

I didn't quite understand why God wanted me, because I remembered how I use to live before Christ came into my life. I was **self** centered, **selfish**, and all about **self**. I wanted no children, no husband, and no pets because **I** had no mind to serve anyone but **myself**. **I** wanted to live the single life of a destined Diva. Freedom was **my** fuel and pompous was **my** purpose. If you'd ever had the opportunity to visit **my** place of residence before the crucial year of 1988, which was when **I** received Christ, you would have come to the same opinion of **me** after simply seeing **my** choice of décor and after viewing the pictures that hang strategically placed on **my** walls. The pages in **my** photo albums we filled with **me**, **I** had one wall covered with pictures of **me** in **my** swimsuit layout, another wall covered with **me** in **my** evening gown layout, all designed by **me**. There was yet another wall covered with **me** pictured in photographs with people who were important to **me**, however the pictures were only important and could only hang on **my** wall if **I** were in them also. That is sick isn't it? Yes of course it is. But, thank God for his Grace and Mercy, thank him for his love, his divine will and for opening **my** blinded eyes. God certainly knew how to get **my** attention. For some it could be the loss of a loved one, an incurable disease or a near death experience. In **my** case, it took an isolated prison experience, and years of hindered spiritual prosperity for **me** to finally understand that **my** bowel movements also have a foul aroma, and **I** needed Jesus just like the rest of mankind. Wow! What a revelation, thank God that **I** was lost but now **I** am found, **I** was blind but now **I** see. Glory to God! As **I** look back **now** and see what God has done for **me**, and where he has brought **me** from, **I** am able to laugh hysterically as **my** tickle box is turned completely over every time **I** think about why God would want to use someone like **me**. It tickles **me** to no end when **I** think about how God, the creator of the all things, took the time to lay out a purpose, a plan, and predestined glory for **my** life.

Now as I continue to walk into my destined place, I am persuaded that nothing can stop me and the best is yet to come. So, after experiencing such a wondrous journey thus far, I believe that in our lifetime the one most important lesson that God ultimately wants us all to learn is that we are more than conquerors through Him that loved us. This understanding comes with time and experience as we learn to walk with the Lord and obey His commandments.

When we trust and believe His holy word, we learn by faith through grace and divine manifestations, that there is nothing that shall be able to separate us from the love of God, which is in Christ Jesus our Lord. Therefore, we are empowered to walk boldly into our destined place without fear or hesitation. So my brothers and my sisters, if death couldn't hold Jesus down **in** the heart of the earth, my question to you is … "What **on** earth can hold you down?"

Let's explore Psalms 23 as it relates to walking with purpose into our destined place.

Psalm 23
¹The LORD is my shepherd; I shall not want.

Well, amen The Lord **is** my shepherd; I shall not want, but what does "I shall not want", really mean? It took me a while to understand what it is, that I shall not want. It took a while because despite what the word of God says, I found myself wanting all the time. Wanting to be successful, wanting to fit in, wanting to be free, wanting prosperity, wanting to be loved etc. However, I now understand that if the Lord is indeed my shepherd, the phrase, "I shall not want" means exactly that, I SHALL NOT WANT.

I discovered that this was possible when I finally delighted myself in the Lord according to ... <u>Psalm 37:4</u> **Delight thyself** also in the LORD: and he shall give thee the desires of thine heart. Also in <u>Isaiah 58:14</u> Then shalt thou **delight thyself** in the LORD; and I will cause thee to ride upon the high places of the earth, and feed thee with the heritage of Jacob thy father: for the mouth of the LORD hath spoken it.

Hallelujah, the Word of God clearly declares that I shall not want when I delight myself in the Lord.

²He maketh me to lie down in green pastures: he leadeth me beside the still waters.

In my mind, this verse in scripture describes my idea of "perfect peace". So, when I think of lying down in green pastures, I see a prosperous resting place where I can gather strength for the duration of the journey. And the very thought of being lead beside still waters by the Almighty God, depicts in my mind the portrait of a peaceful pathway filled with joyous sights. However, after many years of working out my own soul salvation with much fear and trembling, I have come to understand that this is not just in my mind. My life's testimony confirms absolute manifestation of perfect peace, according to <u>Isaiah 26:3</u> **Thou wilt keep him in perfect peace,** whose mind is stayed on thee: because he trusteth in thee. And so, even though the storms keep on raging in my life, I have learned to sing along with my brother, Douglas Miller, the world-renowned lyrics, "My soul has been anchored in the Lord." In other words, I have peace in the midst of a storm because I have learned to keep my mind stayed on Him. Allow me to explain, you see, during one of my seasons, while practicing to live in perfect peace, I was faced many trials. There were some who declared that no one always has peace, especially when faced with trials and tribulations; they told me I should stop smiling all the time and just keep it real. However, I beg to differ, and I submit that it is all in how we think. I choose to allow my mind to be renewed by the Word of God, especially in the midst of trials and tribulations. I choose to think on the things above, which bring me peace, not on things in the earth, which bring me sorrow. In doing so, I have learned that trusting God's Word is as **real** as it gets. I submit therefore that the reason many have argued the genuine nature of my daily joy and dispute the smile that I wear on my face, is because God has given me a gift that is not comprehensible to the carnal mind, the gift of perfect peace according to <u>Philippians 4:7</u> And the **peace** of God, which **passeth all understanding**, shall keep your hearts and minds through Christ Jesus. You see, I believe that there were those and will always be some who simply can't understand this peace because it is perfect peace, an undisputable gift from God.

This scenario reminds me of a song we use to sing in church, back in the day. One verse of that song went like this, *"This peace that I have ... the world didn't give it to me ... the world didn't give it and the world can't take it away."*

3He restoreth my soul: he leadeth me in the <u>paths of righteousness</u> for his name's sake.

Before I submitted my life to Christ, I was given the false impression that once I opened my heart and transformation took place in my spirit, everyday that followed would be blissfully blessed. I was lead to believe that the Spirit of God would redirect my life and I would walk proudly in the paths of righteousness for his name's sake, drama free. Well, I soon learned that this was the truth, but only in bits and parts. You see, there was and is much more to walking in the paths of righteousness than I was lead to believe. After he restored my soul, saved me and filled me with the gift of the Holy Ghost, no one told me that the enemy would be hot on my trail, trying desperately to persuade me to forfeit God's purpose in my life. So, please understand that when we live our lives for His name's sake we must be prepared for trials and tribulations, knowing surely, and having unwavering faith that in the end, we win. So, after I understood the phrase, "For His name's sake", I have to say that each trial has made me stronger and more determined to please God with my life; and this is the mystery of how He restores our soul and leads us in the pathways of righteousness. "If this Gospel be hid, it is hid to them that are lost." They that live Godly shall suffer persecution, but in the end, we win.

⁴Yea, though I walk through the valley of the shadow of death, I will fear no evil: for thou art with me; thy rod and thy staff they comfort me.

Knowledge is power and understanding is strength, therefore when we walk through the valley of the shadow of death, or in other words, this thing called life, there is no reason to fear evil. Know that He is with us, and be comforted in knowing that if the same Spirit that raised Jesus from the dead has quickened our mortal body, and the irrevocable Spirit Death couldn't hold Jesus down in the Grave, what can keep us from fulfilling God's will in our lives? We are more than conquerors through Jesus Christ and we have the victory.

⁵Thou preparest a table before me in the presence of mine enemies: thou anointest my head with oil; my cup runneth over.

Whew! This is powerful, and if you would allow me to be transparent concerning my thoughts and feelings about this scripture, I will openly share how it has blessed my spirit along this journey as I continue to walk into my destined place. I have to begin by saying that this particular scripture continuously provokes my greatest spiritual growth challenges. Allow me to explain, you see, my flesh wants to be lifted up in pride and boast about my blessings, because I was once humiliated and mocked. My enemies said I would never accomplish anything and now that God has blessed me and raised me up out of the miry clay, in the presence of my enemies, I have to be honest and admit that sometimes I want to laugh in their faces. Sometimes I even feel like a kid in a candy store and I just want to dance around, stick my tongue out, and sing the "Na Na Na Na Na Song" in the faces of my enemies. Now, I know that all of this might sound funny or even immature, but it is true. Experience has afforded me the opportunity to come into the understanding that when the Lord blesses me in the sight of my haters or prepares a table before me in the presence of my enemies, I must remain humble in order to maintain this graced position.

Even though I encounter a serious spiritual warfare between my flesh and the Spirit each time God blesses me, I now understand that while my flesh wants to be puffed up and gloat as though I did something to deserve this position, the Holy Ghost will not allow me to comfortably live or function with this rebellious behavior. I am constantly reminded that all gifts come from above, and the Gracious

Spirit of the Holy Ghost intercedes on my behalf, in an effort to teach me how to maintain my position of grace and favor.

You may ask, "How does the Holy Ghost intercede for us?" Well according to the word of God, intercession is accomplished through the Spirit by bringing His Word to our remembrance in the time of need, giving us a chance to choose righteousness.

My most profound experiences with intercession have been in the midst of the blissful part of my blessings, which is when my enemies are usually present. This is when the Holy Ghost on the inside of my soul would encourage me to remain humble, to hold my peace, and just be grateful for the blessing. Constantly reminding me that I have done absolutely nothing so special that warrants my worthiness of this blessing, therefore it is wise that I allow the Spirit of humility to minister to my soul, and be subject to the Word of God in a situation like this. Furthermore, the Spirit of God contends with my flesh to make me understand that if I do so, God will exalt me in due season. Well, even though I am a tongue talking, Holy Ghost filled believer, I haven't always been subject to the Spirit in this situation and I have to be honest and admit that it is not an easy task to remain humble and walk in the Spirit of humility when receiving a blessing in the presence of my enemies; this is why I say that this scripture provokes my greatest spiritual growth challenge. Imagine receiving a long awaited blessing from God in the presence of your enemies, the very enemies who laughed in your face, mocked you and boldly declared that you would never accomplish anything, "What would you do, and how would you respond?" Hmmm? That's something to think about isn't it?

Be encouraged my brothers and my sisters because I have found that when you take the time to weigh the eternal blessing that comes from obeying the Word of God against the weight of the temporary glory of laughing in your enemy's face, the eternal blessing produces a far more exceeding and eternal weight of glory.

I discovered this revelation when I began to question the Lord about the apparent stunt in my growth. You see, even though God continues to bless me, I realized that I was not moving to new levels nor experiencing heavenly bliss, it felt like I was merely going around in circles. Can you believe it actually took almost seven years for me to finally understand what was hindering me? The Holy Ghost revealed to me that the error of my way was my inability and unwillingness to walk in humility after receiving a blessing from God. And furthermore the Spirit of God rebuked me, created in me a clean heart and renewed a right spirit within me. It was then that I finally took the humility challenge and unselfishly refused to yield to the desires of my flesh by walking in self-exaltation and pride. As a result, God has blessed my life to move to new dimensions and to enjoy spiritual and natural bliss like never before.

'Surely goodness and mercy shall follow me all the days of my life: and I will dwell in the house of the LORD forever.

Praise God! For his goodness and for mercy toward us, for it is because of his mercy that we are not consumed by the affairs of this life. His compassion does not fail, and his mercy endures forever, this is why we, the children of God, the royal priesthood, the peculiar people, God's elect, can boldly declare that goodness and mercy shall follow us all of the days of our lives and we will dwell in the house of the Lord forever.

Hearing the Voice of God – Divine Direction

Hearing a Divine word coupled with instructions from God concerning your life's situation can be a very enlightening encounter; particularly when you feel like no one cares or understands your personal dilemma. In fact, if you have ever been favored to have this kind of divine experience with the true and living God, I am sure you would agree that there is nothing in this world that compares to hearing a simple word from God; especially when your life is in the midst of an emotional storm. When you know for certain that you have heard a word from God, no one can dispute it or deny it, because it is an explosive experience that cannot be duplicated or replicated in any shape form or fashion. It is Heaven on Earth. However, after experiencing this kind of personal attention from God, one can begin to feel very special, unique, set apart and even lifted up in pride, as if they did something to deserve God's mercy and grace. Please understand that even though we are indeed special and unique in God's eyes, it is important to remember that the sun still rises in the east and sets in the west, and we have nothing to do with that transaction.

Ephesians 2:8-9

8For by grace are ye saved through faith; and that not of yourselves: it is the gift of God:

9Not of works, lest any man should boast.

Now having said that, and even though we feel like Kings and Queens in the Kingdom of God, we should obey and be encouraged to humble ourselves under the mighty hands of God. Each time we experience a victory we should learn to rejoice without lifting our spirits up in pride. If we do so, God will continue to bless us and keep us as we walk the pathway into our destined place.

Jeremiah 13:18
*Say unto the king and to the queen, **Humble yourselves**, sit down: for your principalities shall come down, even the crown of your glory.*

James 4:10
***Humble yourselves** in the sight of the Lord, and he shall lift you up.*

1 Peter 5:6
***Humble yourselves** therefore under the mighty hand of God, that he may exalt you in due time:*

Now, on the contrary, after experiencing a divine intervention from God, understanding that God apparently cares for us; if we begin to assume that we are better than others in any way, presumptuously or openly, God is sure to fix the situation, but only because he loves us.

Proverbs 13:24
*He that spareth his rod hateth his son: but he that **love**th him **chasten**eth him betimes.*

Hebrews 12:6
For whom the Lord **loveth** *he* **chasteneth**, *and scourgeth every son whom he receiveth.*

Revelation 3:19
As many as I **love**, *I rebuke and* **chasten**: *be zealous therefore, and repent.*

God the Father will continue to bless us and keep us; nonetheless He will also break us again and again until we learn the simple lesson of how to present our bodies as a living sacrifice, holy and acceptable unto God, which is our reasonable service. Here is one simple scripture that can help us reach that goal.

John 15:12
This is my commandment, that ye love one another, as I have loved you.

Understanding this will not only help us to please God, but it will teach us the crucial lesson of life, that the blessing and breaking process is all part of the divine plan and will of God to prepare us along the journey as we walk into our destined place.
TO WHOM MUCH IS GIVEN MUCH IS REQUIRED
New Levels, New Devils – Great Trials Greater Triumphs

Luke 12:48
...For unto whomsoever **much is** *given, of him shall be* **much required** *...*

What does "much required" really mean? I believe it means the greater the trials the more extraordinary the triumphs. When I inquired about the meaning of those words, my understanding came as a result of a whole new journey filled with experiences that were apparently designed to open my eyes concerning the nature of my call into the ministry. You see, I thought that after all I had been through I had suffered enough. I said, "Self, you have been through the storm and the rain, and you are still here, so it is time for God to release the blessings in your life, now." However, I soon learned that the Prophet Isaiah was telling the truth when he declared the word of the Lord saying:

Isaiah 55
[8]*For my thoughts are not your thoughts, neither are your ways my ways, saith the LORD.*

This simply means, God's time is not our time, because his thoughts are not our thoughts, neither are his ways our ways. And just when we begin to think that we've got God all figured out and we've been through enough, and simply can't take anymore, we are faced with yet another trial. Please know that the trial is not what's important, however our response to the trial is critical.

MATURE RESPONSE to Trials
Produces EVIDENCE OF Spiritual GROWTH

I will share a very intimate situation that I had to deal with concerning my physical health, and I will share with you how I responded. You see this was a whole new battle field for me, because most of my trials, as you have read in prior chapters, had primarily taken place in events that would destroy my mind and tear down my credibility as a woman of God. I had not suffered with any physical problems concerning my health, and I wasn't looking forward to any. So, after all that I had been through, prison, a broken marriage, spiritual manipulation, rape etc., and when I realized that I was still standing after these series of storms, I thought I had been through enough suffering for God to just open up the windows of heaven and pour me out a blessing that I would not have room enough to receive. But then, just when I thought I could see the dawning of a new day, I was in the shower singing praises unto God, when I discovered a lump in my breast the size of a quarter. I panicked as these two deadly words ran across my mind, "breast cancer". I immediately stopped singing as I breathlessly pressed my back against the shower wall and slid slowly down to my knees in a defeated posture, and angrily said, with tears in my eyes, "Oh my God, haven't I been through enough?" "Damn, I didn't go through this much hell when I was in the world, serving Satan". I am sure that we can agree that at times, Satan causes many of us to think like this, but it is a lie.

Have you ever wondered what it would be like to be saved, sanctified and living with total chaos all around you? Of course not, why would anyone think like that. It doesn't make since, right? Traditionally we believe that once we give our lives to Christ, everything will be a bed of roses, but more commonly, the truth is when most of us finally made the decision to come to Christ it was not because we loved and adored Him so much, this is why it is written in **Isaiah 53: 2, 3**

"... he hath no form nor comeliness; and when we shall see him, there is no beauty that we should desire him, He is despised and rejected of men; a man of sorrows, and acquainted with grief, and we hid as it were our faces from him; he was despised, and we esteemed him not."

So in the midst of this situation that I was facing, I asked God, "Do trials, tribulations; sufferings and persecution have an end?" And then, the Holy

Ghost began to minister to my soul, right there in the shower. He began to bring scripture after scripture to my remembrance saying, "Yes all things under that sun have an end, but ...

2 Timothy 3:12
Yea, and all that will live godly in Christ Jesus shall **suffer persecution.**"

I said, "God, when will the blissful blessings materialize in my life?"
He said,

Hebrews 10:36
For ye have **need** *of* **patience***, that, after ye have done the will of God, ye might receive the promise.*

I said, "Lord, do you really love me?"
And the Holy Ghost said ...

John 3:16
For God so **loved** *the* **world***, that he gave his only begotten Son, that whosoever believeth in him should not perish, but have everlasting life.*

I said, "Lord, I believe this is true, so please open my eyes and help me to see life the way you see it, then help me understand salvation and the benefit of suffering for your names sake?"
Then the Holy Ghost began to minister to me saying ...

2 Timothy 2:12
If we **suffer***, we shall also* **reign** *with him ...*

Hallelujah!

THE CO$T

Who would have ever thought that the anointing would cost so much, I mean didn't Jesus pay it all? Why do we have to suffer? Why can't we just confess our sins, be renewed by the Spirit of God and live in Heavenly bliss and prosperity for the rest of our lives? We deserve it, right? Wrong, in fact if God would reward us for our works, for our disobedience and for even our thoughts, we would all die. Salvation means to be made free, rescued or recovered, delivered from or given a way of escape. So, even though the way has been made, we must work out our soul salvation by incessantly using the tools, the gifts, faith and the divine instructions that have been freely given to us.

So now, even though I was communicating clearly with God, on a first name basis in the shower, the lump was yet in my breast, wreaking havoc in my mind as I imagined lying in a hospital bed face to face with death. Shucks, I imagined chemo-therapy burning the growth follicles from which the hair on my head grows, slowly destroying my glory. The imagination of my mind had already made funeral arrangements and buried me in the grave before I even finished my shower. As fear gripped my heart with strong hands, I heard another voice in the midst of this storm saying ...

Psalm 118:17
I shall not die, but live, and declare the works of the LORD.

Psalm 103
¹Bless the LORD, O my soul: and all that is within me, bless his holy name.

²Bless the LORD, O my soul, and forget not all his benefits:

³Who forgiveth all thine iniquities; who **healeth all thy diseases;**

⁴Who redeemeth thy life from destruction; *who crowneth thee with lovingkindness and tender mercies*

Now, even after hearing those encouraging words from God, I still had to face the trial and go through the process. Well, like most people, I didn't want to go through the process alone and even though I was confident that God was with me, I still wanted someone to hold my hand and believe God with me; so without hesitation, I called my ex-husband. Now, you may be wondering why on earth she would call her ex-husband. Well, as I reflect on the series of events that followed my call to him, I too, wondered why on earth I called him. Please allow me to explain. You see, even though we had gone through a bitter divorce, and we were in the midst of a child custody and support battle, I still believed that he would be willing to provide me with emotional support through this ordeal, I mean he was my husband for ten years and the father of my only child, Why wouldn't he support me? So, I set an appointment for a mammogram and invited him to come along, and he gladly accepted my invitation. Now, even though he seemed a bit over anxious to know the results, there was no reason for alarm in my mind. I couldn't fathom in my mind the reasoning behind his anxiety, because I wasn't anxious at all. Needless to say, I soon found out why he was so eager to hear the results, as his desire was exposed when anxiety got the best of him. He decided not to wait for the results from the doctor, because he was so sure that the results were positive. You see, he believed, without doubt, that my test results would definitely read positive for cancer, because this would serve as my punishment from God, for leaving him and the church where we fellowshipped. That is sick isn't it? Of course it is. Why would anyone look forward to watching someone suffer with cancer? (*Let me stop for a moment and Breath deeply*) Ok...At any rate, his inability to keep my medical condition in confidence was revealed to me when I happened upon a sister from the church where we attended. I was in a supermarket when the sister walked up to me and began expressing how sorry she was to hear about my unfortunate medical condition, yes, the same medical condition that I, the patient, was still waiting to hear the results for. In other words, she was sorry to hear that I had breast cancer, but I didn't even know if the results were positive yet. Can you imagine how I felt? Shucks, I was already going through enough turmoil while waiting for the results from the doctor's lab. So, I was hurt, I felt humiliated, violated and above all, I was angry. I stood there speechless as she embraced me while saying, "I will keep you in my prayers, and God is a healer".

I thought to ask her where she gathered her information about my condition, however, I already knew that it was highly unlikely that she had received a divine revelation from God about my condition, therefore, there was only one other source ... yes, my ex-husband. After realizing this, I was so angry and hurt that I just gritted my teeth, trying desperately to be cordial as I stood there in this awkward position is dismay. Then I managed to muster of the strength to say, "thank you", as I walked away holding back my tears. Nonetheless, after taking a few days to think about my conversation with this sister in the supermarket, I decided that it would be best if I didn't say anything to him about it. I just didn't have the energy to fight with him, and frankly it didn't matter to me anymore, I was tired. I didn't want to be bothered with him anymore, and I was saddened to know that I had confided in a man who harbored a malicious desire in his heart to see me suffer with cancer. I couldn't understand why he hated me so much, was it because he loved me? Was it because things didn't work out between us? Why so much hate? Anyhow, I did not to invite him to go back to the doctors with me to finally get the real results, because he had already offensively predicted my fait. Nonetheless, he called me several times to let me know that he would meet me at the doctor's office. When I arrived at the doctor's office, he was already in the parking lot, sitting in his car waiting for me. We went inside; I signed in and we sat in the waiting room until the nurse called my name. I have to admit that sitting there with him was very awkward for me because, he was expecting a positive result, while I believed God for the opposite.

He had already told other people about my condition, while I was sitting there still waiting for the results. So I had nothing much to say to him during the wait. When the nurse finally called my name, he jumped up out of his seat preparing to go back to see the doctor with me. I quickly reminded him that we were no longer married and he had lost his spousal privileges, so he could just sit back down and wait until I came out, or he could leave and call me later. Well, as you can imagine, he was not going to leave because he was too anxious for the results. So, I followed the nurse into the patient care room, and sat there reluctantly awaiting the results as I experienced a flood of mixed emotions. Nonetheless, I was confident that no matter what the results were, I was prepared to deal with it. So, when the doctor came in, greeted me, and sat down to open my file with the results, I was ready. She opened my medical file and read my test results which were **negative**. She went on to explain to me that the lump in my breast was **benign,** meaning (not cancerous) Hallelujah!

As I sat there in the patient care room, after the doctor had read me the real results, I began to praise God for his mercy. Meanwhile, my ex-husband was still sitting in the waiting room anticipating the results. I girded up my thoughts, thanked the doctor and walked out into the waiting room where he was sitting. When he saw me coming, he immediately stood up and began walking in my direction. I could tell that he was trying to read the emotions on my face; however my emotions were screaming the opposite of his expectation. So, he said, "Well what's the result?" I said, "The results were negative, I do not have cancer." Well, a normal response from someone, anyone who cares, would have been a praise statement like "Hallelujah", "Thank God" , "Praise Jesus" or simply "I am so happy for you", but instead of him rejoicing with me, he said and expressed the unthinkable "What?" as if he was shocked or disappointed. So, I repeated, "The results were negative, I do not have cancer." He said, "So the results were negative?" As if he couldn't believe what I'd said. Then finally he gathered the strength to say, "That's good" and then he hugged me. At this point I was very happy about the results but I was hurt, because it was apparent that he was looking forward to a positive cancer result. I was his wife for ten years and the mother of his only child, I couldn't fathom in my wildest imaginations, why he would want to see me suffer with cancer? Well, it didn't matter to me anymore, I had better things to do with my life than to sit around and wonder why someone else wanted to see me suffer or fail. God had shown his mercy and I was prepared to move on in pursuit of my dreams, goals and Gods divine plan for my life.

After this traumatic ordeal, I was ready to walk into my destined place without fear or hesitation. This is when I vowed that I would use every gift that God gave me, to glorify the name of the Lord. As a **mother**, I vowed to raise my daughter in the fear of the Lord, teaching her by example to exalt his name and to obey his word. As a **minister**, I vowed to always take the opportunity to share the Word of the Lord and win souls for Christ. As a **playwright**, I vowed to creatively bring to the stage, real life changing messages that minister to the very heart, steering away from illusions and lies that create false hopes and dreams. As a **praise-dancer**, I vowed to dance in the Spirit with authority under the anointing of the Holy Ghost, to provoke a praise and worship atmosphere in the presence of the Lord, no matter what the arena. As an **author**, I vowed to write the truth, share testimony, and expose the enemy, so that as others read, they will be empowered to live victoriously in the name of Jesus. As a **designer**, I would create unique items for Gods special people who were created in his image. And after all of these things, anything else that God would so desire to use me to do, I am willing and ready.

Life is precious, and so I will let nothing stand in the way of my mission, understanding that nothing can stop what God has ordained.

Jesus did his part by dieing so we could be free, and now we must stand fast and walk in the liberty wherewith Christ has made us free.

You see, walking is a continued action word, and as I continue on this pathway of walking into my destined place, facing new challenges everyday, I constantly remind myself ...

Romans 8:28 (KJV)
28And we know that **all things** work together for good to them that love God, to them who are the called according to his purpose.

Chapter 7
BEHIND THE SCENES and ON STAGE

IS THAT MAN YOUR HUSBAND?

They the told me I couldn't do it, they said I couldn't write, they even said I shouldn't try ... Who are they? They are liars, because the word of God says ...

Philippians 4:13
I can do **all things through Christ** which strengtheneth me.

Everyone who says "I am with you" or "I've got your back" is not always telling the truth. So, don't be turned inside out when people quit or are unwilling to work with you. If God is for you, he is more than the whole world against you, and if he gave you a vision, he will provide. So, let me tell you, whenever someone tells you that you can't do something, it is a lie.

I embraced the courage to write, by simply making the choice to trust the Word of God and ignore discouraging words from liars. Listen, my brothers and my sisters, if you are you a dreamer who is gifted with the tools to see your dreams come true, don't allow yourself to be stripped of your strength by haters and jealous folks? Trust me; these kinds of people do exist in places you would never imagine, for example you may have run across them amongst people that you thought were your close personal friends, your co-workers, your family members or unbelievably even among those that profess Jesus Christ to be Lord and Savior. But, be of good courage because you have already overcome, and **God's gonna to bless you**. Does that line sound familiar, well it should, if you saw the play. You see, it is the famous line delivered by the *Prophet Doc Booker*, a character from my play, also titled "Is That Man Your Husband?" This character was derived from a combination of ministers whose delivery of Gods word was always dramatized and charismatic, even comical to me; yet their words were effective and sharper than a two edged sword. Any how, my reasoning for writing the *Prophets* famous line, **"Gods gonna bless you"**, to be delivered in a comedic format in the play, was because those words have seriously blessed and encouraged me over the years. When I first understood that it was and is God's good pleasure to bless me, the phrase, **"Gods gonna bless you"**, afforded me the opportunity to laugh at the calamity of my enemies moving purpose driven into my destined place without fear or hesitation. Especially in the presence of those who continue to smile in my face, greet me with the sacred phrase, **"Praise the Lord, Sister"**, and then talk negatively about me behind my back, as if I don't know it. I once heard someone say, "She thinks she is all of that", and when I realized that they were talking about me, at first I was baffled because I didn't know exactly what "that" was. Anyhow, I don't know about you, but I am still trying to figure out just what "that" is, exactly. At any rate, I am what God says I am; "more than a conqueror" and the mere words of lying perpetrators do not move my emotions nor do they shake my boots in the least bit, because I would rather fail at doing something, rather than succeed at doing nothing.

If you will allow me to define my positive attitude, in an adverse situation like this, I would submit to you that, my joy is enforced because I know the truth. You see a person who speaks negatively about me or anyone who endeavors to do something positive with their gifts and talents, are only portraying a negative image of self, and are motivated by jealousy, because the bible says ...

Proverbs 23:7
*"For as he **thinketh** in **his heart**, so is he ..."*

Therefore, I am encouraged and careful to speak positive, life giving words, especially when I am faced with a conversation that includes someone's character or something that I am not particularly fond of.

Encouragement and excitement tend to be my reaction when I discover that my name or my works have become a topic for discussion among liars, because I understand that breath is too valuable to waste. So, if people choose to talk about me, I must be doing something that warrants the breath of life. Now, I know this may sound strange or even border line sarcastic to learn that someone would be encouraged or even excited about being negatively discussed on any level; however, I am delighted to announce that I am absolutely energized! This overwhelming positive energy comes from knowing that my life and my works are in God's hands; and together we are making an impact among those who have not yet discovered their purpose.

HOLDING ON TO YOUR DREAMS

What ever you do, please find your way into the place that God has prepared for you. Let nothing stop you. Don't ever let go of neither your faith, determination nor your desire to go after your dreams; but rather be encouraged. Although dreams begin as mere thoughts, imaginations or ideas that seem unrealistic or unreachable at times; please understand and know for certain, that our dreams are definitely attainable realities when we have the nerve to encourage ourselves and trust God.

FAITH WITHOUT WORKS IS DEAD

If we believe God, we should just simply step out on faith and begin working toward building our visions and dreams, right? Well yes, of course, but not without wisdom.

Luke 14:28

For which of you, intending to build a tower, sitteth not down first, and counteth the cost, whether he have sufficient to finish it?

His Grace is sufficient in all things and his strength is made perfect in our weakness. I discovered this stunning revelation after I heard from the Lord and without fear, began running with the vision that he had given. He said **"write"** and I began to put pen to paper.

WRITING THE PLAY

When I first heard the Lord say **"write"**, honestly I was excited to hear from the Lord, but I didn't know where to begin because I had so many things toiling in my spirit. I didn't know if he meant for me to write a book, a play, a movie or just a note; nevertheless, I was certain that I had heard from God. I remember falling down to a prostrate position, in the middle of the floor in my unfurnished apartment, with a desperate need to feel the presence of the Lord. And while I lay there, feeling like a complete failure because of all

I had been through and failed at, I began to cry out to the Lord for direction. I didn't know what to do with myself and I had a critical need to hear a word from the Lord. It was then in the midst of my tears, I heard the Lord say, **"write"**. Let me testify that just one word from the Lord can turn your whole life around. When I got up from the floor, dried my weeping eyes and finally sat down in front of my computer, which had become my companion, I began to write like never before. I had no direction and no thought pattern, but I was unmistakably writing by spiritual inspiration. I found myself writing passionately about what I was feeling, intensely about what I was thinking; freely about things that I never thought I would be able to share with anyone, and humorously about how I had overcome. I wrote about situations and circumstances that occurred in my life and in my marriage. Writing soon became a frequent outlet for me to release the pain and anguish that I had held inside for so long, in fact it was therapeutic for me. Weeks had past and I was still writing everyday, like in a journal; except I was not writing about things that I was presently dealing with or encountering, I was writing about past experiences in my marriage and in the church. Then the day soon came when I had "the phone conversation" that changed my whole life. (The one that I told you about in Chapter one)

THE TITLE "Is That Man Your Husband?"

Wow! This simple question was so profound to me. In fact, when my special friend asked me this question, it stirred something in my spirit, and created a fire like none that I'd ever experienced before; a fire that is still burning bright today.

I had no idea that the material I had written in my journal could someday become the content

that would answer this simple question **"Is That Man Your Husband?"** In other words, this question soon became the title for my "now" national hit Gospel stage play and best selling book; both of which have changed my life for the better, forever.
Now let's go...

BEHIND THE SCENES
IS THAT MAN YOUR HUSBAND? THE PLAY

ACT I
Scene I   **The Dupree Home**
        Song: Is That Man Your Husband?
Scene II **Let's Go to Church**
        Song: Married and Lonely too
Scene III **Trouble in Paradise**
Scene IV **The Bar**
Scene V **"Special Project"**
        Song: Beautiful

ACT II
Scene I   **A New Season Chardonnay's Home**
        Song: Chance
Song: Wedding Plans
Scene II **Let's Go Back To Church**
        Song: Love Your Wife
Scene III **Darrell (the Mail Man) Goes Postal**
Scene IV **Cold Feet**
        Song: Understanding I do
Scene V **The Wedding Scene / Finale**
        Song: Cause I am still in love
Song: Reprise - So In love

The Characters
    I've already told you about the Prophet Doc Booker, and where his character was derived from, so now, let's unveil our leading lady character, **Mrs. Chardonnay Dupree**. "Chardonnay", in my opinion, is a beautiful and sexy name for wine. I thought this name would be perfect for this character

because it is a depiction of the writer; a simple, beautiful young woman, who was confused and looking for love in all the wrong places. I named her Chardonnay because even as a person can become drunk and dysfunctional when under the influence of wine, the truth behind the nature of this character is that she was drunk and dysfunctional under the influence of a man's persuasion over her life.

The character known as **Devante Dupree;** portrays the alter ego of my ex-husband. There were times when I didn't know if he wanted to be a preacher or a playboy. I had previously nick named him, *"The bible toting Casanova"*. Although that particular title fit his character perfectly, I needed to give the character a name in the play. So, as I delved into my mind, trying desperately to come up with a name that would fit this character, I kept coming up blank. Then, during a conversation with an old industry acquaintance, he blurted out the name "DeVante Dupree" and needless to say... I thought it was perfect. The name "Devante" had the sound of an innocent young boy from the ghetto, while the name "Dupree" encompassed the overtone of a want-to-be playboy. Both of these descriptions perfectly depicted my ex-husband, and this is how and why this name was adopted for this character.

Angel, is a character that was comprised of several different women who had been like *Angels* of encouragement to me over the years. There was always one who made me laugh even in the midst of tribulations; and others who made me cry because they would tell me the truth without regard for my feelings. This is why the character named "Angel" portrays the image of a best friend, a confidant, and an example of a woman who is happily married.

The **Pastor**, this character portrays an image of a Pastor or leader who believes and functions as if the sun rises and sets on his back side. This character was definitely written to be comic relief. Let's face it, the very fact that someone would even dare to think that they are the center of God's purpose in your life, is comedy within itself. Writing this character with a comedic overtone is my way of sending the clear message of freedom, because I am now able to laugh when I remember all of the hurt that I suffered in the church, at the hand of the Pastor/Apostle. Please understand that this character was not written in the spirit of mockery, but in the spirit of liberty. Believe me when I tell you that there is nothing like being hurt in the church, but there is **absolutely** nothing like being able to get over it and then moving forward with your destined life.

Momma Hump-King, this very zany character is an exaggerated overtone of my mother. She portrays the kind of mother who never bothers in her children's business. However, she will, without hesitation, and with boldness, voice her opinion to whoever, whenever, about whatever. There are times when I sit and talk with my mother about the issues of life, and each time my dad's name is mentioned or something is said to bring his name to mind, my mom has a moment of reflection that literally brings tears to her eyes, even though my dad has been with the Lord for over twenty years now.

Darrell, "The Mail Man", this character exhibits several different men who were in my life at one time or another. There was one who was secretly in love with me, and another who maliciously tried to destroy every possibility of my ever engaging in a serious relationship with anyone besides himself. What better way to depict this character than in the likes of a mail man.

Kelly, also known as "Sunshine" is a character that was developed to portray the alter ego of a *sister*, from my past, who possessed a very raunchy spirit. This sister was the epitome of deception. When you look upon her face and listen to her words, you would think she was sold out for Jesus and walking in the anointing power of Christ. She was a petite, young, well dressed woman; who would soak herself with a very popular perfume, topping off her innocent look with a pleasant smile. The excessive use of perfume and the smile definitely exposed the effort put forth in her attempt to cover that ferocious body odor and that deceitful spirit that she carried. I would have never thought my husband would desire to lay with her, because he and I often had conversation about the foul aroma that she carried. Her stench was so strong that it would literally find its way out from underneath her heavy application of perfumed diamonds, literally taking your breath away. When I found out that my husband was exchanging body fluids with her, I was speechless. He would tell me that he was going out for a ride, or to get an apple from a nearby super market; when in fact he was going to lay with his mistress.

So, in the stage play, when *DeVante* tells *Chardonnay* that he is going for a ride; in my depiction of these characters, I lead him straight to the bar, which is the typical place to pick up a woman with that kind of raunchy nature.

While writing the script, I decided to redeem this character, and she receives Christ through the witness of her fictitious mother.

Malcolm is also a fictitious character who exists only in my dreams at the present time. Therefore I will wait patiently on the Lord until my dreams become a reality.

THE PLAY / THE BOOK

Wit and creativity has made expressive writing pretty enjoyable for me. And even as other great writers, I also write from my personal experiences. However, for me, writing is how I express my liberty as I boldly stand in the place where Christ has made me free.

In this book and in the play, I have freely written about my personal life challenges, pitfalls, triumphs and victories, with hopes that someone will be inspired or encouraged.

In the play, I was able to write from a fictional perspective with a foundation based on truth. However, in the book I was able to just simply tell the truth.

PRODUCTION CHALLENGES

During my journey of producing the play (Is That Man Your Husband?), I found out that the script remained in tact while the cast continued to change year after year.

At first I was troubled by this, because I fell in love with my first cast and I wanted our relationship to continue. You see, they had played an intricate part in helping to make my dream of producing a play come true. I was so pleased with their performance that I wanted to keep them all, forever. Needless to say, I had a lot to learn about business, ministry and becoming a producer. One of the most valuable lessons I learned on my journey, was the priceless lesson called "Change".

THE POWER OF CHANGE

Change promotes growth, growth produces quality, and quality edify's success.

In other words, if we don't change, we won't grow, and if we don't grow, we can never possess the quality that produces success.

I thank God for giving me the courage to accept change, because it has afforded me the opportunity to travel and work with many richly gifted and wonderful people over the years. There were some who took advantage of my weaknesses, and then there were those who saw my potential and chose to stand in the gaps for me. At this point, I could write an additional seven chapters about all of the self serving people who hurt me along this journey; however, I have chosen to share a more positive and enlightening experience about a man that I call "my Angel".

MY PRODUCTION ANGEL

Until this point in the book, I have purposely not mentioned real names in order to protect identity. However, in this segment, I must call my Angel by his name, because I want the world to know who this wonderful man is and how gracious he has treated me from the first day we met, until now. He is by far one of the most humble men I have ever known, and I count it a privilege and a pleasure to have been blessed to make his acquaintance. His name is *Lanyard Williams*.

When I first met this phenomenal man, it was when I decided to step out on faith, book a theatre, and produce my first ticketed stage play, titled **"2 Faces"**. After I had overcome the tedious task of booking the venue and after I had finally figured out how to jump over the hurdle of raising the funds to pay for this event, I walked boldly into the theatre to meet my assigned technician, Lanyard Williams.

The purpose of our meeting was to discuss the tech rider for the show, which consisted of lighting and sound needs for the show. Believe it or not, I had no idea what the role of a theatre technician was, not to mention that he would need a script, a lighting plot, and a sound sheet in order to help produce my show. Furthermore,

I had no idea what a "set" was, nor did I know how to properly place props; I only knew that I wanted to put my show on the stage.

Unmistakably driven by vision, I walked into the theatre as if I had just taken home a *Director of the year award*. Nevertheless, even though that couldn't have been further from the truth, at that time, my angel *(Lanyard Williams)* never made me feel otherwise. I began to give direction, aggressively telling him what I wanted and how to set up the stage. Although he had been working in theatre for twenty plus years on all levels including writing, producing, directing and technical, he humbly listened and heeded to my every command. After looking back and reflecting on that particular experience of working with him, I realized that working with me had to be quite a task, and *Lanyard* was apparently on divine assignment. He demonstrated the highest level of humility in my presence as he had to figure out everything that I was requesting for my show and then interpret my requests in a language that the other technicians could comprehend, because I had no knowledge of technical theatre terminology.

In light of all of this, there is one moment that stands out clear in my mind and moves me to tears every time I think about the unassuming nature that *Lanyard* displayed, in order to help me. Allow me to share. You see, I was in the process of setting up the chairs on the stage for my church scene. And as I set forth on the mission to figure out how to place the chairs in the scene, when *Lanyard* saw that I was struggling with placing the furniture in the right place, he never said one word nor made one gesture to make me feel incompetent. But rather, he stood back and watched me through eyes filled with wisdom and waited patiently for the opportunity to assist me. In my ignorance, my final placement of the seating for the church scene would have placed the actors/actresses in position with their backs to the audience, just like in a real church. Needless to say, if you know anything about theatre, you know that this is definitely not the way the stage should be set up. The actors should always face the audience, so that no expression is missed. When my production angel, *(Lanyard)* saw my ignorance in operation, he graciously allowed humility to rule his actions and wisdom to charge his words as he asked me, what I thought about turning the chairs for this scene to face the audience. In my ignorance, I uncompromisingly said, "No, I want it to look like a real church". Lanyard, then walked down from the stage, sat in the audience, and kindly asked me to sit in one of the chairs in the church scene to show him what the actors would be doing. As I sat down in the chair with my back to the audience, I felt awkward because I could not effectively show him what the actors would be doing without turning around to face him. It was then, that I realized why I should turn the chairs in the scene to face the audience, but that was all I realized.

One would think that after an episode like this, I would realize that I didn't know what I was doing and furthermore that I needed some help. However, it was quite the contrary; instead of humbling myself, I responded by saying, "Ok, that's a good idea, I will turn the chairs around", and then I took over again, as if it were my idea. Was I proud or arrogant? No, not at all; just very excited, determined and driven by vision.

REALIZATION

This might be hard to believe but, I didn't realize how much *Lanyard* had helped me until seven years later, someone asked me questions about my theatrical education. I paused for a moment as I reflected on where I had actually learned all that I know about theatre production. It was then that the tears welled up in my eyes as I finally realized that God had blessed me with my production Angel, Lanyard Williams. Today Mr. Williams is one of my best friends and is an exceptional person in this book because of his kindness and wisdom.

THE PAST

The most challenging part of writing the play and the book was actually having to re-live some of the most painful and degrading events of my life. However I was able to triumph with victory when I realized that I was actually free and willing to put intimate pieces of my life's story in a book and share it with the world. I pray that as you have read this book, you were inspired, enlightened and encouraged to walk boldly into your destined place. Fear and hesitation should be a thing of the past.

ENCOURAGMENT FOR THE FUTURE
Hebrews 11 (Old King James Version)

1Now faith is the substance of things hoped for, the evidence of things not seen.

2For by it the elders obtained a good report.

3Through faith we understand that the worlds were framed by the word of God, so that things which are seen were not made of things which do appear.

FAITH HEROS
5By faith Enoch was translated that he should not see death; and was not found, because God had translated him: for before his translation he had this testimony, that he pleased God.

6But without faith it is impossible to please him: for he that cometh to God must believe that he is, and that he is a rewarder of them that diligently seek him.

7By faith Noah, being warned of God of things not seen as yet, moved with fear, prepared an ark to the saving of his house; by the which he condemned the world, and became heir of the righteousness which is by faith.

8By faith Abraham, when he was called to go out into a place which he should after receive for an inheritance, obeyed; and he went out, not knowing whither he went.

11Through faith also Sara herself received strength to conceive seed, and was delivered of a child when she was past age, because she judged him faithful who had promised.

17By faith Abraham, when he was tried, offered up Isaac: and he that had received the promises offered up his only begotten son,

29By faith they passed through the Red sea as by dry land: which the Egyptians assaying to do were drowned.

30By faith the walls of Jericho fell down, after they were compassed about seven days.

31By faith the harlot Rahab perished not with them that believed not, when she had received the spies with peace.

So ... If you have a dream or a vision, I encourage you to work towards acquiring what you see. Remain focused on the vision, trusting God all the way. Focus is the motivator to get you to the finish line of the journey to make your dreams a reality. Although the way is made for the faithful and the diligent, never get so caught up with the vision, that you disregard the journey that leads you through. Learn from your mistakes and remember that seeing the vision is only the first facet. Know that building the vision is another ball game all together. Understand that it is a common thing on the journey of vision building, to face many trials and tribulations. This will help you to avoid discouragement. And finally realize that often time's, our trials and tribulations are the tests that prove and prepare us for the vision. So, if we keep moving toward vision in spite of the obstacles, it is **also** a very common thing to experience triumph. Sometimes you might have to walk alone, but things work out for the good of them who have faith and love the Lord.

DREAMS DO COME TRUE ...
BUT first, we Must WAKE UP!

The End

SONGS FROM THE PLAY
1. Is That Man Your Husband?

Lyrics: TITLE SONG
Chorus: *Is that man your husband*
Lead: *Some say that time will tell*
Chorus: *Is that man your husband*
Verse I - Lead: *Some say that time can tell, but even though time can tell, time won't fix it, just won't fix it ... cause when you marry the wrong*

man, in the beginning you don't understand, you just take him by the hand, believing that you will stand ... stand the test of time, but in your heart and in your mind, nothing was really clear, you just wanted a man near.

Chorus: Is that man your husband
Lead: Some say that time will tell
Chorus: Is that man your husband
Verse II - Lead: Some say that time can tell, but even though time can tell, time won't fix it, just won't fix it ... Now as time keeps passing by, you begin to realize, that something just aint right, cause (all the time) you've got tears in your eyes, you call upon the Lord asking, "what went wrong", the Lord replies "My daughter, you didn't wait, you found him on your own
VAMP –
Is that man, Is that man, Is that man your husband

2. Married and Lonely Too

Lyrics:
Verse 1
When I dream of marriage, and how it should be,
Two people coming together, to share their love forever,
Standing by each others side, to lend a shoulder when we have to cry,
To wipe the tears from each others eyes, it helps release the pain inside, But ...
What do you do, **when you're married and lonely too?**
Verse II
When I dream of marriage and how it should be,
I long for my companion to hold me closely,
Oh! The comfort of his touch, from the man, I love so much,

To have someone special with whom you share,
Knowing there is someone who cares, But …
What do you do, **when you're married and lonely too?**

   3. Beautiful – *Written by: Fredrick "Jabari" Wright*
(The lyrics of this song were originally to encourage me during a trying time in my life)   Thank you "Jabari"
Lyrics:
Verse 1
Don't be discouraged Sister, have courage and you'll find that broken hearts will heal in time.
Sister, please listen to the voice inside, allow it to personify, let the whole entire world witness your light.
See he's a savage man, below average man, he abuses you, he don't understand the real value of a woman.
BRIDGE
He isn't worthy of your love, but your worthy and deserving just because….
CHORUS: *You're beautiful*
Lead: *Not only physical but deep within your soul*
CHORUS: *You're beautiful*
Lead: *Even in the darkest hour like that moon light you glow*
CHORUS: *You're beautiful*
Lead: *Mere words cannot describe exactly who you are*
CHORUS: *You're beautiful*
Lead: *Divine you shine much brighter than a star*
BRIDGE
He isn't worthy of your love, but your worthy and deserving just because….
Verse II

I know he didn't treat you right, let this be a lesson, but don't lessen your drive to win
You've got to go on with your life, to deprive yourself of living, would be a sin
Don't you even worry about him, he's gonna get it, when the getting is no longer good.
And the same law that gives him hell, will give you heaven, if you only believe that it will.
VAMP - You're beautiful

4. Love Your Wife (as Christ Loved the Church)
Lyrics:
Verse 1
The time is now, the day has come, for you to come together, and be as one ... No more fooling around, those days are done
And when the enemy, starts knocking on the doors of your heart
Know that his only mission is to tear you apart
Rebuke him in the name of Jesus, He's the only one that can help save and protect you love Oh!
Keep Jesus, in the center of your heart,
Satan will never be able to tear you apart
Keep Jesus in the Center and Oh!
CHORUS: Love your wife, Love your wife, Love your wife
As Christ Loved the church
Verse II
Be lovers, be friends, always respect one another
Know your place in his life, not just as his woman but as his wife
(God will bless you and you can walk in the light)
And when the enemy, starts knocking on the doors of your heart
Know that his only mission is to tear you apart
Rebuke him in the name of Jesus, He's the only one that can help save and protect you love Oh!

Keep Jesus, in the center of your heart,
Satan will never be able to tear you apart
Keep Jesus in the Center and Oh!
CHORUS: *Love your wife, Love your wife, Love your wife*
As Christ Loved the church
VAMP – MINISTRY *– Marriage Counsel*
(You've got to take care of her in sickness and in health, for richer, for poorer, forsaking everyone else) Love Her, Love Her...

5. Chance

Lyrics:
Verse 1
I remember the day, I remember it well, you answered the door,
I delivered your mail.
Your smile, worth every mile, though my visits were short,
they were worth my while.
Over and over for you, I thank God, though my chances with you, were against all Odds.
I dreamed of taking you, in my loving arms, and sharing a romantic dance
I dreamed of taking you, in these loving arms,
All I needed was a chance, all I needed was a chance,
Just a chance, just a chance, just a chance, just a chance
CHORUS; *Chance, chance, chance, chance*
Break Down with the funky beats on the Bongos
All I needed was a Chance.

6. Understanding "I DO"

Lyrics:

Verse 1 – Momma

When you say the words "I do", they've got to come straight from your heart

When you say the words "I do", its gotta be 'til death do us part

And your hearts got to be fixed, and prepared to go through, so the next time you standing at the alter, be sure you understand the words when you say "I do".

CHORUS: I do ...... I do

Verse II - Chardonnay

I thought I understood the words, when I said I do,

I even thought the love that I once shared, was strong enough to carry us through

I wasn't worried about situations that may rise,

had no concern about the tears I might have to cry,

I was prepared to go through

Because you and daddy taught and I thought

I understood the words "I do"

CHORUS: I do ...... I do

Verse 1 – Momma

Your daddy and I counted up the cost, (cause)

The love we shared was special, we didn't want it to be lost

We came together to share our lives

His desire to be my husband and mine to be his wife

Then God blessed us with you (after a few years)

He gave us them brothers of yours too

All in the name of love, we made it through

Because we understood the words "I do"

CHORUS: I do ...... I do FADE OUT

7. Wedding Plans

Lyrics: Duet
Chardonnay: The time has come, to make my wedding plans
Angel: This time you've got yourself a real good man
Chardonnay: He'll be there for me, he'll hold my hand
Angel: Girl I'm so happy, you've got yourself a good man
Chardonnay: my wedding will be a special day
Angel: Don't forget about the Honeymoon
Both: Time to Play

Breakdown

Chardonnay: We've got to pick out the flowers
Angel: We've got to pick out the bows
Chardonnay: We've got to pick out the colors
Angel: and the paint for them toes
Chardonnay: Don't forget about my dress
Angel: and the Tuxedos
Chardonnay: the guest list
Angel: invitations and the list goes on and on
Chardonnay: my wedding will be a special day
Angel: Don't forget about the Honeymoon
Both: Time to Play

Breakdown

Angel: We've got to pick out the time of day
Chardonnay: Don't forget my march in song
Angel: we got to pick out your lingerie
Chardonnay: and my Panty Thong...
Angel: we don't have much time to get it done
Chardonnay: (you're right) we don't have too long
Angel: the cake, the ice cream and the list goes on and on, my girl (Chardonnay is getting married) and ...

Both: We want the whole wide world to know ...
Oh Yeah!

8. Cause I'm Still in Love with You

Lyrics:

Verse 1

I know what's going on in your heart
And our lives were never meant to live apart
I never meant to break your heart
CHORUS: *Cause I'm still in love with you*

Verse II

I heard about the tears in your eyes
So I sat, and asked the Lord why
See I never meant to make you cry
CHORUS: *Cause I still in love with you*

Verse III

I know about the hurt you suffered before
Cause I didn't want to open my hearts door
But that's no more, Girl
CHORUS: *Cause I still in love with you*
FADE....

Other Songs from the Original Sound Track (Not featured on the DVD)

Meet Him at the Well
Cover Me
Who Am I?

MS. MICHELLE PRODUCTS
*THE STAGE PLAY ON DVD
*ORIGINAL MUSICAL SOUND TRACK
FROM THE PLAY
*THE AUDIO BOOK ON CD INCLUDING:
(BONUS MUSICAL TRACKS)
*DIVINE TREASURES UNDERWEAR COLLECTION
LOG ON TO

www.MsMichelle.com
For details

Ms. Michelle Products are available at discounted rates for special quantity bulk purchases for sales promotions, premiums or fund-raising. Book excerpts can be used to create special promotional items to fit specific needs

For details, write to: Marketing Specialist, 500 Elizabeth Avenue North Las Vegas, NV 89030

Printed in the United States
57651LVS00006B/198

9 781425 938208